how to do creative placemaking

An Action-Oriented Guide to Arts in Community Development

National Endowment for the Arts

Table of Contents

Chapter 6: Arts + Community Development Organizations

OFFICE OF MANAGEMENT AND BUDGET
THE WHITE HOUSE

Claiborne Avenue, one of New Orleans' central arteries, traces the Mississippi River and passes through a patchwork of distinct neighborhoods. Just a few blocks off Claiborne you'll find the Saenger Theatre, the largest historic theater in the city. The beloved landmark was greatly damaged in 2005 after Hurricane Katrina caused massive water damage to the theater's interior. After a strong show of interest and support from the local community, followed by an eight-year restoration, the venue was restored to its original 1927 design. The restored theater represents the crown jewel of Canal Street, the "Broadway of the South", and serves as a monument to New Orleans' recovery efforts following Hurricane Katrina. If you step outside you can see the canal streetcar line pass by and the infamous Basin Street, a cultural crossroad that inspired many jazz and blues recording artists in the 1960's.

While today I serve as the Director of Office of Management and Budget, I am also an architect. I understand that our communities are more than just the sum of their parts, stone and steel, concrete and glass, roads and buildings, homes and offices. A beautifully-restored theater, an island of green space, a lively well-lit street, all foster a sense of place and civic culture in one's community.

No city in America sees the intersection of culture and vibrancy like New Orleans. After decades of declining economic activity, the City decided to create a unified approach to planning and redevelopment along Claiborne Avenue. The Mayor's Office of Cultural Economy developed what it called the Claiborne Corridor Cultural Collaborative, or C4, designed to bring the communities together with a shared vision for Claiborne Avenue as a continuous cultural landscape. With a grant from the National Endowment for the Arts' Our Town Program, the City created a mapping tool for community residents to provide data about cultural and economic activities, identifying opportunities for the arts to become a catalyst of economic activity and new housing options for the area.

Like New Orleans, many communities across our country face complex challenges, shaped in part by the fiscal constraints, political pressures, and environmental challenges of our era. I've spent my career working to address such challenges with an eye on the ingredients for thriving, dynamic communities that make opportunity available to all. I have had the chance to delve deeply into the importance of improving and preserving affordable housing for future generations. I know that what makes a neighborhood is more than planning, bricks and mortar. We need the arts to illuminate and surface creative solutions to the challenges of our time. The arts encourage analytical thinking, foster widespread community participation, engagement, and understanding around issues that affect each of us in the places we live, work, play and grow.

President Obama once said "The arts are what make life worth living." The President's leadership has brought federal agencies together in an unprecedented way to create new pathways for local vision to shape and revitalize communities. Coming together to make our communities more lively, beautiful and resilient through the arts surely makes them places worth living. The arts are a powerful agent of community transformation. They can re-kindle a spirit of love for one's community, and can serve as a force for civic cohesion and development, allowing the best of a local community's vision for their future to emerge.

This compilation of essays and case studies demonstrates the powerful role of the arts in breathing new life into downtowns, neighborhoods and rural communities, and connecting people to one another. With the leadership of the NEA, artists and arts organizations are connecting with community leaders across the domains of public health, housing, economic development and beyond. Arts-based community development strategies are playing an essential role in Administration efforts such as Promise Zones, engaging artists as critical contributors to new forms of economic and social capital.

The arts create new ground for citizens to come together to revitalize their communities. With intentional investment and integrated thinking, a bank, energy company and music organization can collaborate to bring a series of pop-up performances to suburban Maize, Kansas; artists, community organizations, scientists and city planners can work to engage citizens of Indianapolis through physical installations along the river to enhance awareness of the waterway and river-related issues affecting their lives. There are many more examples of creative partnerships in these pages which give a glimpse of a future full of new possibilities. I'll leave you with this mosaic of stories and insights in the hope you paint your own beautiful picture of how the arts make life worth living.

Sincerely,

Shaun Donovan
Director

How This Book Is Organized

THE BOOK IS LAID OUT TO HELP YOU easily navigate the creative placemaking topics you might find interesting. Each section has a series of essays from some of the best minds in this field, and also some case studies of projects funded through the NEA's signature arts and community development program—Our Town. Use the Our Town case studies to expand your imagination on what artists and the arts can do to impact community. Here's how to think about what's in each chapter:

Chapter 1

Inclusive Planning + Equitable Development

Planning is one of the first steps in any community development process. Did you know that artists can help enrich a planning process and make it more inclusive—and maybe even fun? Yes, it is possible to have no more boring public meetings! This chapter helps outline how to do that, and also sets the context of what it means to engage creative people to prevent displacement of residents and instead build equitable communities.

Chapter 2

Economic Opportunity

Wondering how to bring back Main Street with arts activities, or how to do a cultural district, or what it means to support artists as small businesses? Perhaps you are from a rural community and are wondering how the arts might help drive economic development? This chapter is for you.

Chapter 3

Community Identity + Belonging

America is a large and complex place with many diverse cultures, many of which have been oppressed or misunderstood for years. In this chapter, the authors explore the issues surrounding how to respectfully and authentically engage the culture of a community.

Chapter 4

Arts + Government

One of the more interesting recent trends in creative placemaking has been the willingness of government to engage the arts to solve a whole host of community issues. In this chapter you can read about artists working on flood preparation, policing, public housing, and more, as well as read about best practices and ways to partner with government on creative placemaking projects. This chapter also describes how the arts help define a community's soul and how artists play a key role in that process.

Chapter 5

Arts + Physical Infrastructure

The physical buildings, public spaces, and artworks that creative placemaking produces are some of the most visible and well-known types of projects in this field. In this chapter we give the basics on cultural facilities, artist housing, public art, and space for creative businesses.

Chapter 6

Arts + Community Development Organizations

Community and neighborhood development organizations are some of the most important players in the revitalization of our communities, as they are typically deeply rooted in a place and its future. Hence, we've dedicated a whole chapter to examples of how these organizations are doing this work, and essays on how their field is adapting arts practices into its policies.

The book concludes with an essay by Maria Rosario Jackson on moving toward a sustainable practice of creative placemaking.

So How Do You Do Creative Placemaking?

BY JASON SCHUPBACH

SO YOU'RE A MAYOR WHO WANTS TO make your city better, or you're a resident of a neighborhood where development is out of control, or you work at a community development organization and are trying to improve the plaza where kids play and folks meet up, or you work in a small town and want to improve Main Street, or you work in a planning or economic development office and are trying to find new ways to engage the public in a project. Since you care about making your place better, you follow the current thinking in planning and community development, and you've been hearing a new term—creative placemaking. What is that, you say? Something about the arts? You love the arts, but what do the arts have to do with making your place better? You want to know how to do creative placemaking.

This book is for you.

In 2009, the National Endowment for the Arts (NEA) decided to focus on the role of arts organizations, artists, and designers in making better places and decided to call it "creative placemaking." It's a term that basically means giving the arts a seat at the community development table. In other words, when you are focusing on a new real estate development, transit opportunities, safety issues, public health crises, or other issues that impact how a place affects a resident's life, the arts should be one of the tools you consider using. You might know how to work with housing finance tools, or road engineering tools, or zoning—this book is to help you understand what are the tools for arts-based community development. It's a primer, and a scan of where some of the best thinking is in 2016. It's meant to help get you started.

WHERE DID CREATIVE PLACEMAKING COME FROM?

The idea that artists, designers, or arts organizations have a role in shaping a community is as old as human civilization, and it has been happening in America for years. In 2010, the National Endowment for the Arts wanted to put an emphasis on building greater support for this type of work, so we did several things. We started by paying some smart folks to do research about where the field of arts in community development was in the country, and named the field "creative placemaking." The idea was to put a policy frame around a set of current activities so that we could research and support the work in an organized way. We then looked at a three-pronged investment strategy of support. The first was the NEA's (really the American people's) money—that became the Our Town program. Our Town funds collaborations between local governments and arts organizations to do projects to improve their communities. The second strategy was new private philanthropy dollars. The former chairman of the NEA, Rocco Landesman, assembled a number of national foundations to create a ten-year (2010-2020) funding and research collaborative called ArtPlace America. Finally, the last strategy was to access and promote arts-based practices in other federal agencies—that's a complex puzzle and we've had lots of successes, as evidenced in the opening letter of the book.

NOW AND THE FUTURE

So the NEA is six years into this adventure—where do we stand? We've now given more than $30 million for 389 Our Town grants in all 50 states, Puerto Rico, and the District of Columbia. ArtPlace America has invested in projects in 43 states and the District of Columbia, and we have all kinds of exciting federal collaborations in the mix.

More importantly though, we are trying to help people learn more about how to do this work in an authentic way. The past six years have definitely taught us that any work done in the complex systems of communities is difficult for anyone, maybe even more so for artists and arts organizations. Also, creative placemaking work exists in (and sometimes is blamed for the negative consequences of) the larger issues shaping our society around race and inequity. The good news is that between the federal government and foundation partners, a lot of energy exists around helping all different kinds of organizations and systems learn arts-based community development tools. There are new investments in everything from opera singers to transportation engineers, all of which are trying to learn more about what it means to do creative placemaking projects. There are efforts to figure out how to get the arts more plugged into other fields that impact communities— safety, public health, housing, transit, etc. And there are efforts to figure out how to sustain creative placemaking work in the long term. We can't wait to see what we all learn on this journey together.

All community development is hard and creative placemaking is no exception. We applaud the folks out there trying to do it, and hope that this book will help some of the curious get a better grounding in the basics of the work. Remember, creative placemaking is really just creative humans trying to help other humans live a better life. This statement might sound cliché—but if you are interested in pursuing arts-based projects in your community, and go forward with an open mind and respectful heart, you will be able to make positive change happen.

The future of your community is up to you.

Jason Schupbach is the director of Design Programs for the National Endowment for the Arts (NEA). In this role, he oversees all design and creative placemaking grantmaking and partnerships, including Our Town and Design Art Works grants, the Mayor's Institute on City Design, the Citizens' Institute on Rural Design, and the NEA's federal agency collaborations.

Chapter 1

inclusive planning + equitable development

How Creativity and Culture Can Contribute to Community Planning

BY LAURA ZABEL

ART AND CULTURE ARE UNDERUTILIZED assets in community planning and development. Working with artists can help improve stakeholder engagement in planning in a number of ways and contribute to plans and developments that represent and serve the people who live in a community.

ARTISTS BRING PEOPLE TO THE CONVERSATION

In community planning and development there is a well-understood need and desire to get input from the people who live and work in the community itself. Community plans have a better chance of being useful, equitable, and healthy if the people who actually live in the community are represented in the planning process. Artists can help organizers and planners transform community-input sessions from lightly attended meetings in musty basement rooms to vibrant, engaging celebrations that invite more diverse participation and input. For example, the Friendly Streets Initiative, a community-led planning and organizing group in St. Paul, Minnesota, successfully worked with a group of artists to design creative and fun block parties where neighbors were invited to give feedback about traffic calming and bike and pedestrian issues in their neighborhood.

ARTISTS IMAGINE THE POSSIBILITIES

Sometimes it can be hard to imagine a different future for a place. Residents and stakeholders can get stuck seeing the challenges facing a neighborhood rather than the assets and opportunities that exist. Artists can help people visualize possible futures for a place, designing community planning processes to translate their hopes and dreams into policy and action. For example, in Fergus Falls, Minnesota, artists have been working for more than two years to design creative projects that connect to the

Community members participate in creative community planning activities.
PHOTO BY
JONATHAN PAVLICA

historic preservation and reuse of the Kirkbride, a former state mental hospital. The issue of what to do with this historic and enormous property had become contentious and emotional for the community. By partnering with community development and historic preservation leaders, local artists have been able to establish themselves as key partners and allies, using their creative skills to engage their neighbors in imagining possible futures for the building and community. Now, after years of community division, there are many more residents at the table and together the community has changed the narrative of the building's future. The Kirkbride is now on the verge of a renaissance. Plans are in the works to convert it into a hotel, apartments, and restaurants. Art and artists have been a core part of the redevelopment.

ARTISTS HIGHLIGHT AND SUPPORT EXISTING ASSETS
In the past, community planning has not always fully recognized the existing assets of a place. Sometimes large development projects were implemented without regard to the potential displacement of people and businesses from the surrounding

community. For the most part, cities and planners recognize that this has been an inequitable approach and now look for ways to implement planning that encourages development without displacement. Many places are implementing new Community Benefit Agreements[1] and other policy interventions to support this goal.

Artists can help planners develop projects that support and celebrate the unique and important strengths of a community that are already in place. For example, during the construction of a new light rail, the Irrigate project in St. Paul engaged artists to create hundreds of small projects in partnership with local businesses and community groups. These projects helped local small businesses and cultural assets to not only survive the construction but also build their capacity to thrive post-construction as the train attracted new development to their neighborhoods.

> Artists can help planners develop projects that support and celebrate the unique and important strengths of a community that are already in place.

ARTISTS CAN PROTOTYPE AND EXPERIMENT

Beyond helping people see that things can be different or better in their community, artists are good at "getting to the doing"—trying small experiments that help test new ideas. Often community organizers and other stakeholders are understandably focused on trying to stop bad things from happening to a neighborhood that can lead to an atmosphere of distrust between city planners and residents. In addition to supporting this work to stop the implementation of inequitable or ill-conceived development, artists can also help organizers and neighborhood groups mark their place, express their voice, and make change in productive, creative (and fun) ways. Often these can be small, low-risk projects that can happen quickly, without the need for long planning processes. For example, the St. Paul Frogtown Neighborhood Association has worked with neighborhood artists to develop "Lot Squats"— performances, installations, and gatherings that allow residents to try different creative uses for the vacant spaces in their neighborhood, "engaging neighbors in discussions about what these lots can be—and how we can reclaim our space."

[1] A Community Benefits Agreement is a legally binding contract (or set of related contracts), setting forth a range of community benefits regarding a development project, and resulting from substantial community involvement.

Julian Gross, *CBAs: Definitions, Values, and Legal Enforceability* (The Partnership for Working Families, January 2008)

ARTISTS HELP BUILD MOMENTUM

The distance between a community plan and actual changes for a neighborhood can be long, particularly with affordable housing development. Often a new development is announced and then (because timelines for big capital projects are lengthy) there is a long period of time where the site is fallow and it appears as if activity has stalled. Artists can help community leaders and developers fill this gap and build energy and momentum. For example, Minnesota-based Project for Pride in Living (PPL) worked with artists to design projects that invited neighbors onto the future site of PPL's new development, which includes 108 new units of housing, retail, and public plaza space. It invited people to engage in creative activities and conversations that asked them to express their definition of "home." These projects provided ongoing activity and physical changes to the site, giving the site a sense of momentum and vibrancy even before any real construction started. They also provided opportunities for neighbors to express their own ideas of home and build a sense of community ownership of the site while being a positive reminder that this new development is not only a physical structure but also people's homes.

YOUR ARTISTS IN YOUR PLACE

Artists are in every neighborhood, on every block. Artists are people who know place, love place, and will use their creativity to tap into its potential and opportunities. An invitation to artists to use their creative skills to support their own neighborhood can help develop and implement plans that are authentic, vibrant, and just, reflecting the community's shared vision for its own future. The Housing and Urban Development office of Community Planning and Development lists as one of its guiding principles, "Planning and execution of community development initiatives must be bottom up and community driven." To enact this principle effectively, planners and developers need creative and culturally relevant strategies that engage diverse and representative stakeholders.

Artists are people who know place, love place, and will use their creativity to tap into its potential and opportunities.

Laura Zabel is executive director of Springboard for the Arts. She has a background in theater, arts leadership, and community development, and is a frequent speaker on arts and community development at convenings such as the Aspen Ideas Festival, International Downtown Association, and Americans for the Arts.

Equity in Practice: Strategies from Alternate ROOTS' History of Creative Placemaking

BY CARLTON TURNER

SINCE 1976, ALTERNATE ROOTS' network of artists has been leading the charge for arts as a conduit for the development of healthy communities in the United States South. During that time, our artists have been developing performances, creative interventions, and cultural organizing practices that foster equity and justice while making art that grows out of communities of tradition, place, and spirit. Our members use their art as an entry point for communities to voice their ideas and thoughts on the challenges they face.

Over the past few years, the rapid pace of gentrification as a form of economic development has become a primary concern of our constituents. Too often, communities become invisible throughout the planning, design, and development process, as these processes are often designed and built by development entities using corporate practices that negate community input. As a result, this work is driven by economic indicators and is largely disconnected from the needs of the existing communities and residents.

Equitable creative placemaking employs practices that center on understanding how power, access, and resources can be used in the service of justice. In this work, justice is the acknowledgment, support, and empowerment of existing communities throughout the development process. In pursuit of justice, we must expand our understanding of creative placemaking beyond economic indicators to include practices that improve people's ability both to live and share space together, and to imagine and then build more sustainable, equitable communities for themselves and future generations. In my 14 years with ROOTS, three cornerstones of equitable creative placemaking have continually risen up; I offer them here, as a grounding for thinking about your own creative placemaking work.

**Performers of *Cry
You One*, in which
audiences participate
in this performance
about Louisiana's
disappearing coastal
communities.**
PHOTO BY
MELISA CARDONA
PHOTOGRAPHY

1. **Recognize and respect cultural "dark matter" as a
   community asset.**

   Many astrophysicists believe that the universe is held
   together by a substance called "dark matter"—it cannot be
   seen or measured but makes up the majority of the mass
   of the universe. In creative placemaking, dark matter is the
   stuff that holds a community together—like history, memory,
   and relationships. It is impossible to measure and is often
   overlooked in development initiatives. However, without
   this dark matter, a community cannot function.

   Very few new development projects are happening in
   communities that are void of people or history. What makes
   culture bearers, artists, elders, and historians integral to
   community development is not only their understanding of
   how and why a community works the way that it does but also
   their ability to identify, witness, and translate this history—
   dark matter—into art, creative process, and visioning.
   Culture bearers are those members of a community that

have accepted the role and responsibility of using their creative practice to cultivate connections and belonging, and activate the spirit of the community that holds them accountable. In some traditional spaces, culture bearers are an essential, visible version of dark matter. They are responsible for holding the people's collective story; carrying their gathering, celebratory, and ceremonial songs; and sharing the sentiment of the community through dance and movement. Such input is invaluable and necessary to support strong, successful community development that both honors what exists and paves the way for a positive transition into the future.

Too often the case for creative placemaking is made through economic indicators such as jobs created, property values, and new businesses. These indicators drive investment and serve as benchmarks and measurements of a certain type of success. This focus on economic-driven measurement is problematic, especially in light of the fact that the income and wealth gaps in our country historically divide across racial and ethnic lines, and only continue to widen.

But the community is always there, they are always present—their constant presence, energy, labor, and relationships are part of the dark matter that holds the community together. It is up to individuals and institutions with financial and material resources to make the choice whether to see or not see them. So, in this role of community development, who is seen and is not seen is a choice. Choosing not to see the community in its wholeness, including the dark matter that holds it together, leads to inequitable and unsustainable development.

We must shift the community development process from only engaging an advisory board or team of artists during the implementation phase to working with the creative community from the very beginning.

2. **Engage artists and community members from the beginning.** We must shift the community development process from only engaging an advisory board or team of artists during the implementation phase to working with the creative community from the very beginning. Artists are visionary by definition. They create something where nothing existed. Although we all possess the ability to create, artists operate from their creative center more consistently than others. Being in tune with their creativity allows artists' perspective to be well-suited to operate in the generative phase of the development process.

Just as artists need to be present from day one, the whole community should have access to conversations and decisions related to the development process from the beginning to ensure that the initiatives that are being designed for their homes are in alignment with their needs and consistent with their vision. The more the people running the development processes can work with communities to foster a sense of true ownership in projects that will affect their lives, the more equitable it will be. The community, however it *self-defines*, should be able to influence direction and be empowered to make decisions—in particular decisions that will directly impact their lives.

One example of this, within Alternate ROOTS, is the work of Clear Creek Collective. As cultural organizers in the mountains of central Kentucky, they use indigenous art, folk songs, and storytelling that is very much connected to the identity of their local culture. Through this approach, they offer an entry point for the community to voice their ideas and thoughts on how development happens.

3. **Art and creativity aren't magic, they're science.**
   When I first came to Alternate ROOTS, I wondered why singing and sitting in circles telling stories at business meetings was so important. I wondered why we took breaks to stretch and move our bodies during our time together in groups big and small. As a young artist I did not understand the connection between these practices and our ability to have difficult conversations in large, diverse (in terms of ethnicity, artistic discipline, education, ability, gender, etc.) groups of people from all walks of life.

   Story circles, as taught to me by John O'Neal of Junebug Productions, is a practice that is as old as community itself, often used to equalize power. Using the circle as a space for participatory democracy, where every voice is honored as important, establishes equity. Singing together grounds our breath and collective rhythm so that we can work together in solidarity. Somatic practices—stretching, dancing—remind us of the very scientific fact that we are minds *and* bodies, and that we tend to ignore the latter to the detriment of the former. Understanding this and employing these practices is important when working together to develop collective strategies that will impact the entire community.

Centering cultural practices in the community development process serves equity and access. Void of them, our development initiatives are one-dimensional and lack long-term significance. When utilized, these practices increase folks' ability to live and work together by amplifying their voice and ownership, and by helping them see themselves, their concerns, and their dreams reflected in the process of making their community stronger. When the process of creative placemaking is more inclusive and equitable, when it is focused on living and working together well, the outcomes will be much more likely to reflect these values. All of this is what equity looks like in practice.

Carlton Turner is the executive director of Alternate ROOTS. He has a background in jazz, hip-hop, spoken word poetry, soul music, and nontraditional storytelling. Turner is currently on the board of Appalshop, First Peoples Fund, and Imagining America and, in 2013, he was named to the Kennedy Center Honors Artist Advisory Board.

Understanding Arts and Culture in Equitable Development

BY JEREMY LIU

AS LONG AS SOCIETY HAS EXISTED, art as a form of cultural expression has been used as a tool for social change. Hence, the arts can address social inequities in a myriad of ways. Art engaged in community development imagines a different future and helps enact it. Arts education nurtures the creativity in each of us so that we are equipped to act, building and rebuilding a community's collective will for social change, one person at a time. Art heals so that we can all participate, and then energizes that participation to further bolster the health and strength of a community. The arts help community development approach change with culture-based and culturally resonant strategies that are as empowering as they are effective.

CULTURE AND ART AS AN AGENT IN THE EQUITY OPPORTUNITY
Culture is a deep well of ideas and solutions from which communities draw strength to solve community problems. As introduced at the 2014 Allied Media Conference and further developed and asserted by Roberto Bedoya in his September 15, 2015 opinion piece for *Creative Time Reports*, "Spatial Justice: Rasquachification, Race and the City," art and cultural approaches to community development, like creative placemaking and creative placekeeping, are simply a contemporary recognition of this strength of character that comes from a community's culture. At its broadest sense, equitable development must balance the ideas of change as an inevitable process (placemaking) and community resiliency as a necessary condition (placekeeping). Creativity as manifested through the arts can leverage culture as a resource to make placemaking and placekeeping more effective and equitable. This duality is the equity opportunity.

Community members engaged in a design charrette in Houston, Texas.
PHOTO BY
PATRICK PETERS

Artists work for equity in many different ways. Artists in collaboration or conjunction with equitable community development practitioners might work in a hybrid approach where one brings a creative process to the other's organizational or community process, like community organizing. For instance, a performance artist could align his or her work with the practice of community organizing, finding common ground in their shared dependency on the engagement of the audience be they gallery visitors, theater-goers, or attendees of a community meeting.

In equitable development, art can serve as a risk-taking mechanism. While equity is a prerequisite to all forms of justice—economic, social, racial, environmental, and otherwise—and while forms of equity are valued in and of themselves, equitable development is fundamentally about subverting existing structures of inequity. Art fits into equitable development so easily because it, too, can be about subversion. By giving permission to the unusual, the margins, the subcultures, and the positive potential of nonconforming behavior, art is a pathway to a social imagination that describes what is and what could be. Each act of employing art as a means of suggestion is a way of exploring what should be, a way of exploring our values.

HOW TO EMPOWER ARTISTS TO FIGHT INEQUITY

In all cases, engaging and empowering artists can challenge the status quo structures that reinforce inequity to advance equitable development. Engaging and empowering artists effectively requires cultivating trust, sharing an understanding and reciprocal acceptance of risk tolerance, balancing the separate yet integrated processes of the artist and the processes of community, and relationship-building that involves thinking and doing together as a form of equitable or equity-oriented art practice.

Beyond recognizing art and artists as a resource, and committing adequate resources to supporting work together, community leaders must have an understanding of artistic practice; likewise artists and other cultural producers must understand community development processes. Tools such as the Interaction Institute for Social Change's Pathway to Change™, PolicyLink's Getting Equity Advocacy Results, and the University of Kansas Work Group for Community Health and Development's Community Tool Box are useful frameworks for understanding community development.

To recognize and understand the dimensions or qualities of artists' practice that affect the equity orientation or potential of the artists (or arts and culture organizations or institutions) to contribute to equitable development, I propose five questions for artists to ask themselves:

- To whom are you accountable?
- Where and with whom does your creativity reside?
- Do you have intentions that are aesthetic? Pragmatic?
- How do you understand the integration of your work as disruptive? Normative?
- What is your sense of individual agency and social influence?

These question are not meant to be evaluative or deterministic; they are a means for understanding, for inviting deeper discussion between community leader and artist. No correct answer exists that automatically means an artist will be more or less suited to address inequity.

ART MAKES EQUITY PROCESSES AND PURPOSES LEGIBLE

The ability of art to express process and purpose simultaneously is a key to how art can accelerate equity and equitable development. In other words, art makes community identity, visions, hopes, values, and practices "legible" by representing them visibly in the design, form, shape, practices, and traditions of a place. So much work in the community development field that tackles inequity is pragmatic and mechanical, like creating jobs through small businesses by providing technical assistance and affordable financing. These are important but not "legible" as acts of advancing equity. Or, in the case of affordable housing, which often tries to blend in with market-rate housing or the existing housing stock of a neighborhood but when completed is frequently not "legible" as an equity mechanism. So art has a role to play in expressing form and story together so that purpose and meaning are intertwined.

Art is a resiliency mechanism for neighborhoods and communities facing change that threatens to overwhelm them. Art reflects a community's processes, intentions, and purpose, but it accommodates changing meaning over time as well. Art can reflect a community context while simultaneously and over time engaging in dialogue about context as a community changes. Expressing context as it is remembered and as it is evolves, between past and present and between present and future community members, can generate empathy and motivate engagement. Change is inherently necessary for addressing social inequities as much as change is a part of every community. Art can help grasp this process. Imagination is a critical element in addressing and ameliorating inequity; the failure of imagination contributes to growing inequity. Art asks the questions that have no correct answer, but these are the questions we must ask ourselves as we work toward equitable development.

> **Art is a resiliency mechanism for neighborhoods and communities facing change that threatens to overwhelm them.**

Jeremy Liu is co-founder of Creative Ecology Partners. Liu is an experienced mixed-use real estate developer and chief executive with a unique background in urban and community planning, creative placemaking, and technology programs. He is currently the senior fellow for arts, culture, and equitable development with PolicyLink.

Stitching It Together: Community Planning as Creative Act

BY TOM BORRUP

Diane Horner
engaged participants
in artistic expression
during the 2014
charrette in
Bloomington,
Minnesota, to
develop creative
placemaking plans
for the South Loop
neighborhood.
PHOTO BY
BRUCE SILCOX

I WANT TO START WITH A PERSONAL EXPERIENCE, one where I witnessed how making artwork together under the guidance of an artist can be the critical element to a successful community planning process:

I am watching North Dakota quilting artist Sarah Heitkamp lead an eclectic group of 80 Grand Forks community members through the steps of cutting and arranging fabric into small squares. In April 2015, 18 years after flood and fire devastated this fiercely independent community, residents had put their city back together. Yet at the beginning of this evening community planning session, I sense a piece still missing. Though residents had done the hard and painful work of physical and economic recovery, they seemed to lack joy in building a community together. Along with the quiltmaking, local music and dance group the Lovely Dozen performed while residents assembled their individual squares into one large patchwork. As the work comes together, I sense the shift happening. I am amazed as young and old pass the microphone to explain the meaning of their contribution to the quilt (and to the community). They applaud each other while celebrating their creative achievement.

ARTISTS AS COMMUNITY PLANNING PARTNERS

The above example is just one of many where adding artists and arts organizations to a city-wide planning process can make a pivotal difference. Artists have long been inspired by and provided inspiration for the landscapes we inhabit—reflecting places and conditions, and evoking a wide range of emotions. Canadian planner Greg Baeker wrote in 2002, "The tools of the artist are an essential part of how we imagine cities: through stories, images, metaphors, exploring possibilities as well as critiques."

The contributions of artists he references represent just some of those that communities are beginning to embrace. This article explores tools artists bring to the planning process to engage people of diverse backgrounds, generating richer analyses and more robust options, while they foster more meaningful engagement in decision-making and create greater community ownership. Tools include ways to find shared vision, exercise voice, find expression through song and movement, share stories, and celebrate the making of something new through group process.

AMPLIFYING VOICES NOT OFTEN HEARD

Among the challenges facing the planning profession are how to understand the needs of changing populations and how to meaningfully engage complex communities. Planning scholar Leonie Sandercock describes what she calls the growing cast of "mongrel cities" where diverse populations and people with conflicting interests share space. In such places, she argues, the "politics of voice" become volatile. Who is speaking, and who is speaking for whom, are frequently asked questions. Artists can help disenfranchised community members find and amplify their voices. Using words as well as other forms of expression, artists can elicit individual and collective fears, questions, emotions, dreams, and visions. Theater-maker Dudley Cocke describes his process as one that "utilizes the inherent intellectual, emotional, spiritual, and material traditions and features of a community to encourage individual agency in support of community well-being."

Artists move us to rethink our ways of understanding.

BUILDING BRIDGES

Conflicts among disenfranchised or disaffected residents go beyond land uses, housing, jobs, roadways, infrastructure, or amenities. Misunderstandings and complex cultural and symbolic conflicts enter the picture in ways many planners find hard to understand, let alone accommodate. Meanwhile, planning practitioners find themselves bound by established practices and their own biases as they pull from a limited vocabulary of aesthetic choices, land-use patterns, and ways of involving people in civic dialogue.

If planners are to truly engage with and address the needs of increasingly diverse communities, they must embrace new vocabularies and new partners to build what urban planner Leo Vazquez refers to as their "cultural competency"—understanding how to communicate and function within cultural environments not their own. Planners need more ways to foster dialogue and creative problem-solving across race, class, and other differences. Artists who are part of or familiar with diverse communities can partner with planners as "interpreters" or "ambassadors" to open critical channels of communication and establish more meaningful connections with diverse communities. In neighborhoods where communities of color have little reason to trust city agencies and planners, creating new productive relationships takes time. For two decades, Juxtaposition Arts has engaged teens and young adults on planning projects in their neighborhood on Minneapolis' African-American-identified Northside. They partner closely with the City and have progressively expanded on their youth-led achievements. Their work has grown from murals, public art, bus shelters, and pocket parks to include streetscapes and neighborhood-wide planning for physical and economic development.

ARTIST CONTRIBUTIONS

Artists move us to rethink our ways of understanding. They re-purpose raw materials to create value and beauty, reveal new meaning, and show us how things can function differently. Artists make things that are new or unique, and challenge common ways of seeing and doing.

For decades, community-based artists have facilitated processes for people to learn and make things together. They have honed skills to deconstruct complex issues and to evoke poignant personal and collective stories. Community arts activities—from locally generated theater and mural projects to neighborhood festivals and youth-focused art, dance, and music classes—are more accessible, inclusive, and usually more fun than most town hall meetings. They engage a wider mix of people while providing meaningful and satisfying experiences. Artists' practices can take stakeholders beyond the symbolic to where they learn from each other and make things together. When such practices are integral to the process, they can take planning to the level of co-creation and help neighbors form new relationships with each other and with civic processes and institutions.

Theater artist Harry Waters, Jr. (left) works with New Orleans neighborhood leaders involved with Claiborne Corridor, blue tape marking the outline of the corridor, 2014.
PHOTO BY TOM BORRUP

DOING THIS WORK

My work as a district planner with cities and neighborhoods across the U.S. has involved working with theater artists, choreographers, vocalist/songwriters, visual artists, designers, and others as leaders and collaborators. As artists, they can generate deeper collaborations, help planners and stakeholders alike to understand challenges in new ways, and model different ways of working productively together. My projects range from neighborhood planning in Saint Paul, Minnesota, and Tulsa, Oklahoma, to cultural planning in California, Michigan, Ohio, and North Dakota, to regional heritage planning in rural Wisconsin and Minnesota; from working with neighborhood groups in New Orleans, Louisiana, and Oklahoma City, Oklahoma, to planning with nonprofit organizations from Massachusetts to Oregon. I have seen artists reinvigorate civic engagement and completely turn planning processes on their head.

In downtown Minneapolis, Minnesota, the yearlong Plan-It Hennepin project engaged residents, business and property owners, nonprofit leaders, artists, students, city officials, and others in a series of artist-led workshops. The workshops gave project planners and designers a chance to soak in ideas while stakeholders co-created goals and strategies for the district. Artists also worked with youth to produce videos, photographs, poetry, and radio spots that highlighted stories of and visions for the district. This 2011-2012 cultural district project showcased one way to engage a diverse mix of stakeholders in a complex environment and brought local knowledge to generate deeper public discussion.

In Bloomington, Minnesota's South Loop, a groundbreaking suburban planning project in 2014-15 included a seven-day charrette co-led by artists. Following the charette, the 18-month project commissioned artists to animate public spaces; involved people in a host of exploration, learning, and planning activities; and built social fabric where little previously existed.

LESSONS LEARNED

In conducting creative planning and engagement activities we learned to:

- Provide a welcoming, safe, interactive environment and include food;
- Connect people with each other on personal, professional, and other levels;
- Listen to everyone's story to construct a larger story of shared place;
- Share our enjoyment of community planning and illustrate that civic process can be fun;
- Embrace conflict as part of the dramatic arc of the story of every place;
- Ensure equitable engagement at the right level for each person;
- Demonstrate thinking and action outside the box;
- Coax people outside their comfort zone (within a safe space);
- Draw connections between ideas, images, places, and people previously not considered related;
- Forge a sense of collective achievement; and
- Leave people with new experiences and new friends, and seeing new possibilities.

CONCLUSION

Using fabric, scissors, stories, songs, movement, paint, and other tools, artists bring decades of community-based arts practice that can reinvigorate community planning. They can unleash imaginations, bridge cultural divides, and build a shared sense of individual and group capacity. As the planning profession embraces artists as partners, our communities see renewed visions take shape while they bridge differences and build stronger social fabric—and embrace the joy in working together to build better communities.

Tom Borrup, PhD, is faculty director of the Arts and Cultural Leadership Program at the University of Minnesota and principal at Creative Community Builders. Borrup pioneered cultural asset mapping and leveraging cultural resources for economic development and civic participation.

The Role of Performing Arts in Place

BY JENNA MORAN

THE PERFORMING ARTS CAN HAVE A PROFOUND effect on individuals and communities. One cannot see a performance without having some kind of reaction—be it positive or negative. Listening to music can uplift your spirits or help you to relax. Seeing a play can make you think about issues from a different perspective. Whatever the experience, performances stick with you long after they are over. Think about the last performance you saw. What do you remember? How did it affect you?

Performances can also create a common bond between individuals. Being part of an audience is a collective—a community—experience. Audience members feed off of one another, and performers in turn play off of their reactions. This sense of the collective intertwined with the impact of a powerful performance can be useful when working to strengthen a local community.

In November 2014, the National Endowment for the Arts in collaboration with ArtPlace America held a convening called Beyond the Building: Performing Arts and Transforming Place. The convening brought together national leaders in the field of performing arts to get a sense of the state of the intersection between performance and place. Here are the top five lessons learned from the convening:

1. **Relationships between performing arts organizations/ artists and community must be reciprocal, based on mutual respect, and present both before work on a performance begins and after it ends.** Relationships are central to creative placemaking—relationships between performing arts organizations and artists, between organizations/artists and funders, between organizations/artists and audiences,

 **Taratibu Youth
Association
performing to
a crowd in front
of Mount Rainier
City Hall.**
PHOTO COURTESY OF
ART LIVES HERE

between audiences and place. As such, it is important that
these relationships are built to last, and that the proper amount
of time is given to form these partnerships. Organizations
and their artists must be out in the field doing their work,
interacting with community members in order to learn what
the community needs over time. Through these interactions,
they form relationships not only with area residents but
also with other area organizations—arts and non-arts—and
local government agencies. Based on mutual respect for
each other's work and reciprocal needs, partnerships can
be established that can then lead to equitable community
development.

2. **Authenticity—of relationships, of funding, etc.—is vitally
    important to creative placemaking work.** An organization and
    its partners should not form partnerships or pursue creative
    placemaking projects for the sole purpose of meeting the
    requirements of new funding guidelines or fitting the newest
    funding model. Creative placemaking partnerships and projects

must develop organically—authentically—around a creative idea that responds to a community issue. Each project must be pursued by organizations that know and have experience with the community and place in which the work will take place. Community development goals should already be part of each organization's vision—whether through its incorporation into mission, core values, and/or programming.

3. **Creative placemaking must be equitable for and inclusive of all people—audiences, artists, and organizations alike.** The ultimate intention behind all creative placemaking work is to transform communities socially, physically, and economically into equitable places with the arts at their core. These efforts should actively seek to avoid gentrification and work hard to ensure that the people who helped make the neighborhood what it is today—often artists—are still in place tomorrow. Partners should seek both to reach residents where they live and work and to bring people out of their homes through unique programming. Thousands of ways to do this exist, including holding arts events in vacant lots and local businesses, adding special bus routes designed to make travel to, from, and around arts venues easier, and scheduling performances at varying hours of the day and week (and at various price points) to allow people with nontraditional schedules the opportunity to experience art live. Additionally, support structures need to be established to help artists and under-resourced organizations not only learn how to do this work well but also build their own capacity to be able to continue doing this work in the future.

> Creative placemaking partnerships and projects must develop organically— authentically— around a creative idea that responds to a community issue.

4. **It is difficult to establish a place for the arts at the community development "table."** The typical community development "table" includes land-use, transportation, economic development, education, housing, infrastructure, and public safety. All too often the arts are left off this list. Creative placemaking work is about making sure the arts find a permanent home at the "table." Arts organizations and artists as individuals need to find innovative ways to make sure that their voices are heard and valued in conversations about the future of their communities.

5. **While performances are oftentimes perceived as temporary events, they have lasting effects and can create lasting change.** Performances are only temporary in the sense that an audience experiences a live performance for a finite amount of time. However, that experience is a small part of a larger continuum. It takes weeks to months of preparation to put on even a single performance. On top of this, creative placemaking efforts should align with other long-term organizational programming and local civic activities and dialogues. Accordingly, these "temporary" performances become experiences on which further community engagement can be built. They are points of entry that inspire civic participation at a very intimate level as the stories told resonate with audience members. Through this connection to story, audience members and places can be transformed. Audience members' perceptions of ideas, places, etc. can change due to newfound empathy or understanding. Places can be endowed with new meaning and imagined in new ways. These are the experiences that create lasting, positive relationships in communities.

Creative placemaking can take place anywhere—inside or outside of an organization's building. It does not matter what you call it—outreach, community engagement, creative placemaking, etc. What matters is that the work is being done. According to Colleen Jennings-Roggensack of Arizona State University Gammage, when starting a creative placemaking endeavor, one should always ask, "What do *we* want? What do *you* want? What do we want *together*?" The points of overlap are where you should focus your work.

"Temporary" performances become experiences on which further community engagement can be built.

Jenna Moran is a program manager at National Association of Counties (NACo) in the community and economic development practice area. She handles community and economic development, resilience, and transportation grants and programs, and is staff liaison to the NACo Arts + Culture Commission. She previously worked at the NEA, assisting on the Our Town program.

Working with Dancers and Residents to Plan the Future of a Transit Corridor

TAKOMA PARK, MD

Arts engagement with youth as part of the "New Hampshire Ave: This Is a Place To…" project in Takoma Park, Maryland.
PHOTO BY
JOHN BORSTEL

IN TAKOMA PARK, MARYLAND, NEW HAMPSHIRE Avenue is a commercial and residential corridor that has long been hard to traverse due to its broad, busy roadways. This lack of walkability has hindered local human interactions and connections among residents. Though the area is culturally rich and remarkably racially diverse, its character is dominated not by the cultural vibrancy of its residents, but by this eight-lane traffic artery that primarily serves as a pass-through for commuters. Necessary infrastructure investments and new redevelopment opportunities designed to address this situation have manifested fears of displacement in the community. To address these issues, Dance Exchange, an internationally recognized contemporary dance company resident in Takoma Park since 1997, understood that the community needed spaces and opportunities for cohesive, intergenerational social interaction that reflected its enduring cultural elements and affirmed its values and aspirations.

"New Hampshire Ave: This Is a Place To…" acknowledged the power of artmaking and performance to bring new meaning to the relationships between individuals, communities, and the places in which they live and work. The project approached local needs in two ways: a "traveling" strategy to encompass the length of the New Hampshire Avenue corridor and a "gathering" strategy to draw participants together at the project's central green space. Among the unexpected outcomes of the project was a shift of focus toward building the capacity of city planners and local community members to cultivate and maintain more meaningful and reciprocal relationships with each other through artmaking and dialogue. Accordingly, Dance Exchange has worked with the City of Takoma Park to discover and articulate ways in which Liz Lerman's Critical Response Process (CRP), an internationally

recognized method for giving and receiving feedback which originated at Dance Exchange, can inform a midstream urban planning process.

The early, exploratory phases of the project included preliminary workshops at area schools, senior centers, and adult and teen institutes in an effort to bring a wider circle of creative community practitioners and teen leaders into engagement with area residents. As the project advanced, pop-up events in green spaces built familiarity and relationships with residents; family workshops at the Rec Center focused on intergenerational movement and storytelling; and public artmaking events allowed partnering artists to engage with the people, stories, and experiences of New Hampshire Avenue. This process of iterative engaging and creating led to deeper relationships as well as richer practices and outcomes as the work progressed. Other project activities included a series of interviews and portrait sittings which ensured that the faces and experiences of people who live and work along the avenue had a presence in conversations about the past, present, and future of the place. To create cohesion between all project events, Dance Exchange designed and produced a group of colorful chairs inscribed with the project title which debuted at a one-day, participatory community festival in September 2014. These chairs have become not only the central image of the project but also a platform for community members to express their celebrations, challenges, needs, and goals for New Hampshire Avenue.

Programming conducted within the scope of the Our Town project has set the stage for future activities taking place with support from ArtPlace America. These upcoming and recent project phases have brought Dance Exchange into collaboration with a range of local artists to create a series of multimedia artworks along New Hampshire Avenue, which appeared as an installation during a site-specific intergenerational performance in July 2015. The performance, created in collaboration with New Hampshire Avenue community members as well as participants in Dance Exchange's 2015 Summer Institute, was in part a re-imagination of Liz Lerman's landmark work, *Still Crossing*, and brought together artists, organizers, and community leaders to explore Dance Exchange tools and practices as related to creative placemaking.

The themes of intersection, journey, and legacy inherent in the revisioning of *Still Crossing* provided a unique, collaborative forum for city planners and residents to have deeper conversations about the celebrations, challenges, needs, and goals of a re-envisioned New Hampshire Avenue. By contributing individual and collective stories to the project through dance, music, visual art, and storytelling, community members had the opportunity to connect in ways that transformed perceptions of self and other, fostered a deeper relationship between what was and what is, and advocated for the presence and importance of community faces and stories within city-driven development initiatives.

Arts engagement with community members as part of the "New Hampshire Ave: This Is a Place To..." project in Takoma Park, Maryland.
PHOTO BY BEN CARVER

Chapter 2

economic opportunity

Bringing Back Main Street: How Community Development Corporations and Artists Are Transforming America's Troubled Commercial Corridors

BY SETH BEATTIE

THE GLENCOVE RIBBON-CUTTING CEREMONY doesn't start for another 30 minutes, but people are already starting to pour in. By the time the event starts, curious visitors will be crowded out onto the sidewalks, waiting to see this new approach to live/work space.

The enthusiasm is understandable. The building has stood vacant for 14 years in Cleveland's Collinwood neighborhood. And it certainly wasn't alone. Between 1940 and 2010, Collinwood lost the equivalent of one resident every 56 hours—for 70 straight years. That population loss contributed to an incredibly weak real estate market. As recently as 1999, Waterloo Road—a major commercial corridor—stood 40 percent vacant.

Thankfully, the vision of local artists charted a way forward. The Beachland Ballroom, a music venue, opened in a shuttered social hall, and Waterloo Arts, a socially conscious arts nonprofit, launched soon after. These investments laid the groundwork for Northeast Shores, the neighborhood's community development corporation (CDC), to pursue an aggressive strategy to build up a creative economy.

The organization started purchasing vacant storefronts and houses. They helped artists develop business plans, remedy bad credit, and shore up their finances. One by one, they positioned artists to buy living and work space—at prices as low as $5,000. As artists settled into the neighborhood, Northeast Shores made sure that their presence was financially rewarded; over just five years, the organization supported the launch of more than 300 community arts projects.

The Glencove ribbon-cutting ceremony in the Collinwood neighborhood of Cleveland, Ohio.
PHOTO BY SETH BEATTIE

Building by building, Waterloo came back. Today, commercial vacancy stands at just six percent, and the street is 100 percent locally owned and operated. The market has gotten strong enough that artist enterprises are spilling out onto nearby streets, including at the recently completed Glencove building.

Now Northeast Shores is partnering with Cornerstone Corporation for Shared Equity on the region's first renter equity program. Three vacant brownstones are being converted into 15 live/work units—every tenant has either a storefront or a workspace, separate from their residential space. Artists pay below-market rents, and a portion of that money is set aside in a savings account. After five years of participating in tenant meetings and paying their rent on time, artists are then able to access more than $4,000 in cash, growing to as much as $10,000 after ten years.

WHAT WORKS

No magic formula exists for how this kind of revitalization takes place. There are scores of examples where community investments in artists have not succeeded in shoring up weak markets and others where markets get so strong that artists and other low-income stakeholders end up getting priced out. Still, many culturally oriented neighborhoods have found success, and there are some commonalities among these models.

It's not all about warehouse space. When I talk to people in early stages of thinking about artist space, repurposing industrial space almost always comes up. To be sure, there is a substantial market of artists who are interested in working or living in an industrial loft. But just like members of any professional group, artists don't behave en masse. Multiple surveys of Cleveland-based artists, for example, have demonstrated that about two-thirds are seeking workspace outside of industrial lofts. And when it comes to living space, artists are twice as likely to want to be in a Colonial house as in an industrial building.

> The fastest, most sustainable way to build relationships with arts entrepreneurs is to examine what is already in your portfolio and how it might be better packaged for an artist audience.

It's not all about special services. Similarly, many organizations start off by thinking about what special new programs they can launch to bring artists in. To be sure, special initiatives catering to artist needs are impactful. Often, though, so are a CDC's existing services. In Collinwood, we looked at 28 programs that Northeast Shores already offered and repackaged them with an eye toward artist needs. We found that artists had particularly strong interest in:

- Low-cost homeownership;
- Free or low-cost access to space for pop-up events;
- Assistance in developing business plans; and
- Fiscal sponsorship of community projects.

This work suggests that the fastest, most sustainable way to build relationships with arts entrepreneurs is to examine what is already in your portfolio and how it might be better packaged for an artist audience.

It's not all about commercial activity. Substantial numbers of creative entrepreneurs out there want dedicated places to make sales. Still, the vast majority of artists make only a fraction of income from selling art in a single geographic area. Many earn their primary living in other professions or sell online, or exhibit or tour in multiple cities. Even if they are not ready to sign a lease, engaging such artists can have substantial impacts on commercial corridors. Artists' events can bring new visitors into a neighborhood—or engage residents in a deeper way. Artists can help small business owners refine promotional materials, store appearance, and shopping experiences. And socially conscious artists can address issues that might otherwise hold a street back, such as public safety concerns, lack of pedestrian activity, and vacant storefront windows. All their different contributions together maximize a sense of momentum along a street.

It *is* about narrative. CDCs are called on to do a lot, often with limited staffs, small budgets, and in places where private markets have failed. We simply cannot expect them to be the sole engines of change. Instead, we have to ensure that their investments encourage a broader group of stakeholders to invest their own resources.

To me, the most exciting potential for collaborations with artists is recapturing the narrative of what makes a place worthy of investment. Exploring a place's history, celebrating its culture, and helping people envision an achievable future—that is a place where artists can have immense impact.

In the end, it is why people are standing in line to see the Glencove. All the redevelopment in Collinwood has been important, but it is what is happening inside those buildings that is stoking imagination. Artists in Collinwood are launching hundreds of community projects, proposing creative solutions to everything from obesity to vacant lots. They are encouraging people to reclaim the neighborhood's blue-collar heritage not as a badge of shame but rather as a celebration of tenacity.

Exploring a place's history, celebrating its culture, and helping people envision an achievable future—that is a place where artists can have immense impact.

Local residents are feeling again like they are part of something and that their community is on an upward trajectory. This kind of atmosphere is sustaining commercial development in Collinwood— and across America—and is exactly why even a simple ribbon cutting is a standing-room-only affair.

Seth Beattie is the founder of Spire + Base. He has an extensive background in creative placemaking and community development, including community research, strategic planning, project development and phasing strategy, artist support program development, proposal and report development, and strategic communication strategy.

Using Empty Storefronts as Catalysts for Economic Revitalization

NEW HAVEN, CT

KNOWN AS THE "CREATIVE CAPITAL" of Connecticut, New Haven is the state's second-largest city. With more than 125,000 residents, 11,000 university students, and a greater metropolitan population of 850,000, the city supports several commercial districts, including the historic City Center. After undergoing redevelopment in the 1980s and introducing 311 apartments with ground floor retail, City Center proved to be quite successful as a residential area. However, the retail elements languished, leaving a series of vacant storefronts. When the national recession hit in 2008, the area's already sluggish economy was exacerbated.

To revitalize City Center and attract potential commercial tenants, the city looked to find new ways to increase area foot traffic. Recognizing that while creative activities were thriving—creative industries in New Haven are estimated to employ more than 5,600 people (7.3 percent of the workforce) spread across 440 different firms—they lacked permanent spaces in which to grow, the city's Department of Arts, Culture and Tourism (DACT) developed Project Storefronts, a program that fills empty retail spaces with galleries, studios, and arts-related offices.

Inspired by Los Angeles' Phantom Gallery and New York's Swing Space Program, Project Storefronts offers 90-day, no-rent leases to creative businesses, with the option for successive 90-day renewals. Individual artists/artist teams, nonprofit arts organizations, and for-profit creative entrepreneurs/start-up enterprises with missions related to the arts and the creative industries can apply to occupy and utilize these empty retail spaces in imaginative and innovative ways. Project Storefronts gives them the opportunity to demonstrate viability and tweak their business plans in a low-budget, low-risk environment.

New Haven has six goals for the project:

Storefronts in downtown New Haven, Connecticut.
PHOTO COURTESY OF PROJECT STOREFRONTS NEW HAVEN

1. to create visitor destinations in formerly empty spaces in order to drive new consumers into underutilized areas, increasing foot traffic and business to not only these spaces but neighboring ones as well;
2. to raise awareness of New Haven's different commercial districts and help promote underutilized spaces to potential long-term tenants, which can eventually create jobs and increase the tax base;
3. to grow interest in and awareness of the arts and expand people's understanding and appreciation of creative endeavors;
4. to encourage creativity to blossom and grow in New Haven;
5. to enliven New Haven neighborhoods by expanding commercial activity, making the city more attractive to potential residents, businesses, students, and other artists;
6. and to facilitate artistic, creative, and entrepreneurial businesses.

DACT has approached the project methodically, refining the concept, weighing feasibility, and addressing legal issues. It starts the process by negotiating with private property owners for rent-free leases to existing and new retail spaces and/or reduced or in-kind services; the close partnerships that develop through this process are crucial to the program's success. The next step is to select creative entrepreneurs to occupy the storefronts. Once the entrepreneurs are in place, DACT provides administrative and logistical support to help them in the development of their retail spaces, the procurement of insurance, and the navigation of legal issues. The City's Office of Economic Development (OED) and the Economic Development Corporation (EDC) also help the selected entrepreneurs by providing small business counseling and fiscal oversight.

To promote the program throughout the community and city, DACT organizes public events, including a citywide open studios program, an arts festival, and an exhibition. More than 20,000 people, representing a broad cross-section of the community and city, participate in these events annually. The Ninth Square Merchants Association was created to help organize continued activities around these new and temporary entrepreneurial businesses. As further evidence of its success, the project helped create four new businesses in its first year: Karaoke Heroes, Neville's Fashion Design, Our Empty Space, and Vito's Artmart.

There is anecdotal evidence that foot traffic in the area has increased, viable new retail businesses are taking shape, and community engagement with area residents has increased. Moreover, the project's success is spreading to other Connecticut cities, as Bridgeport (CreateHereNow) and Hartford (iConnect) have both found success with programs similar to Project Storefronts. All in all, a new, more relaxed culture has engulfed the area, and people now see Hartford's City Center as a place to congregate.

The Human-Scale Spark

BY ESTHER ROBINSON

WE AT ARTHOME BELIEVE IN THE POWER of human-scaled change. We also believe that change agents need the right tools to do their work. Testing revitalization tools with artists gives communities a targeted way to build a body of new insights and new approaches, shaping and reinvigorating the process of positive neighborhood change. As creative placemaking continues to gain momentum as a tool for revitalization, it now seems like a perfect moment to look at some of the deeper mechanics of creative enterprise at the neighborhood level.

ArtHome's current project, ArtBuilt Mobile Studios—a program where we provide studio space that can be easily moved to different locations—builds assets and infrastructure support for artists, creative businesses, and the communities in which they reside. Through this and other programming, we have spent more than ten years supporting individuals starting creative businesses and exploring the benefits communities can generate by encouraging small-scale creative enterprise locally.

This work has produced four key insights that have wider implications than the arts:

1. A neighborhood's ability to communicate its unique assets is crucial for its capacity to catalyze positive change.
2. Creatively and economically, a unique neighborhood or regional identity is often stewarded by enterprises and individuals operating at very small scale.
3. Smaller-scale enterprises and individuals are undersupported by traditional business support services.
4. New forms of micro-enterprise support offer a visible and effective way to bring new life to revitalization efforts.

Children performing at ArtHome's ArtBuilt Mobile Studio.
PHOTO BY
ESTHER ROBINSON

In our work supporting low-income artists—whether through Individual Development Account (IDA) match-grant savings, peer-lending and access to micro-credit, financial training, or providing affordable workspace opportunities with ArtBuilt Mobile Studios—we have seen time and again how micro-enterprise art businesses can be radically strengthened by very modest levels of investment. Also, we have seen the transformative effect these small-scale interventions can have on artists' creative output and connection to audiences and markets.

SMALL-SCALE VERSUS "ENTERPRISE-LEVEL" ECONOMIC ACTIVITY
Much existing economic development support for disadvantaged communities—even that which leverages creative placemaking—is targeted at "enterprise-level" economic activity: multi-employee businesses, access to commercial lending, capital and infrastructure funding at levels far beyond the capacities of individuals and very small businesses. We feel that this approach misses out on precisely the type of low-level economic empowerment that most directly affects livability and vitality—the individual and micro-business level.

Economic growth is part of the picture, but most effectively so when it happens from the ground up: when individuals have the tools and resources they need for their activities—creative, entrepreneurial, socially oriented—to thrive and yield fruit in their communities. We feel strongly that identifying and supporting existing creative micro-businesses is a key factor in strengthening a neighborhood's singular character—and that that support can function just as effectively for non-arts micro-businesses, with similar impacts on overall vitality.

BARRIERS TO BUILDING CREATIVE ENTERPRISES

In the environments where we work—disinvested urban neighborhoods on the one hand, and areas where high rental costs are driving significant displacement on the other—we see a set of economic barriers that effectively stifle very small-scale creative enterprises.

Broadly speaking, these barriers are about scale: availability of appropriately sized and priced real estate; access to small-scale lending; and training for business, marketing, and financial planning appropriate to individual/sole-proprietor enterprises. These same barriers affect all kinds of entrepreneurial activity at similar scale—the micro-enterprises, which we believe are the most effective seeds for revitalization, community stability, and social cohesion.

Creative placemaking tends to focus on the cumulative outputs of local creative endeavor: streetscape improvements, anchor venues, cultural activity as an attractor for foot traffic and commercial-corridor spending, and so on. Whether those outputs function as metrics for measuring vitality or are seen as building blocks for ongoing economic development, they tend to eclipse the small-scale, individual activities of creative workers as a functional driver for vitality.

Our notion of how creative placemaking functions is somewhat different: we believe artists and creative workers are attracted to a given neighborhood by the same factors that allow any micro-enterprise to flourish: affordable and appropriate workspaces and a flexible approach to regulatory issues and

Economic growth is part of the picture, but most effectively so when it happens from the ground up: when individuals have the tools and resources they need for their activities to thrive and yield fruit in their communities.

dynamic place-centric activity. Where these conditions exist, creative activity thrives—and so does micro-enterprise more broadly. Where they do not exist, creating them allows for the sort of grassroots vitality that sparks not just creative enterprise, but a broad range of small-scale economic activity that can profoundly change a community's livability. We think much of creative placemaking's broader success stems from precisely this low-level ferment and human-scale spark.

We see real vitality as coming from *within* communities, at local scale, generated by individual members engaging in individual transactions on a personal level.

TOOLS FOR SUCCESS

So how are we putting these insights to work? Our current efforts aim to provide both individuals and their community partners with new tools for micro-business support. Tools which combine the unique properties of individuals and place to strengthen cultural vitality at the neighborhood level. For example, ArtBuilt Mobile Studios are carefully designed, high-quality movable workspaces, providing an appropriately scaled home for micro-businesses in places where no suitable spaces exist. They are highly affordable— well within the means of an individual or small community group to build and own; they are mobile, allowing communities to re-imagine unused and under-used locations as springboards for vitality; they multiply impacts, allowing a single creative producer or service provider to access multiple audiences in multiple locations from the same physical base; and, importantly, they provide a highly visible platform for micro-enterprises, helping communities embrace and appreciate this often undervalued sector, and spotlighting an important conversation about place, vitality, and individual creative enterprise.

We see real vitality as coming from within communities, at local scale, generated by individual members engaging in individual transactions on a personal level.

Esther Robinson is an award-winning documentary filmmaker and producer, and the founder of ArtHome, which provides financial training and asset-building programming to artists and organizations nationally. Since 2015, she has been co-director of the New York City nonprofit ArtBuilt, where she continues ArtHome's asset-building programming alongside space-based artist-support initiatives.

Strategic Planning for Arts, Culture, and Entertainment Districts

BY AMANDA J. ASHLEY

ART, CULTURAL, AND ENTERTAINMENT (ACE) DISTRICTS are an increasingly popular policy tool, marketing strategy, and targeted cultural investment for neighborhoods, cities, and regions in the United States. Public agencies, private groups, quasi-governmental bodies, and community-based organizations experiment with different types of ACE districts, typically with the intent of economic and community development. Districts are created by a variety of different types of people, from individual entrepreneurs and artists to more formal public/private partnerships.

Cultural districts policy is still a relatively young field. It continues to evolve as planners, policymakers, and advocates gain more insight from evaluation, community feedback, and professional convenings. What we do know is that districts have the potential to create and enliven place, to support creative and cultural enterprises, to provide opportunities for community and neighborhood engagement, to attract visitors and outside investment, and to support local workers and businesses.

The district itself is often a contemporary artifact of the community's history and culture, and is an important part of a region's arts ecology. District scale, mix, design, and audience vary considerably and are quite diverse. For example, some districts bring together traditional nonprofit arts activity, including museums, theaters, and galleries. Others feature artisans, artist entrepreneurs, and commercial creative industries. Some support existing neighborhood arts activity and creative community development. Districts also range in their designation and financial models. Some are state or locally sanctioned districts with taxing authority, while others are informal marketing devices driven by volunteer support and grant dollars.

**Ground Control
International Space
Orchestra performing
in Santa Clara County,
California.**
PHOTO BY
NELLY BEN HAYOUN

Districts can be controversial for many reasons. People debate
whether districts are a good use of public investment, whether
they lead to gentrification and displacement, whether they are
manufactured and inauthentic, and whether they lead to new
economic and community growth. It is not always clear if cities
should draw their own districts from scratch or support those that
are market-driven and organic, or if cities and district advocates
have the capacity to create sustained policy, regulatory, and
marketing support as public priorities evolve. These important
conversations should drive communities to consider the goals
and values that they hope to achieve through development of
a district, and how to address challenges as they arise.

All districts succeed in some ways and struggle in others.
The best or most successful districts are those that have developed
capacity—the harnessing of internal and external resources—by
being reflective, innovative, nimble, integrated, and collaborative.
At its core, building capacity helps move district leaders from
hoping and planning to meeting their objectives and goals.

For those interested in building and managing ACE districts, here are six lessons to keep in mind:

1. **Be local:** ACE districts should reflect the history, culture, and place of their locations. No single solution or recipe for success exists. While it is helpful to see how others have proceeded, it is dangerous and ill-advised to follow their same path, as the political, economic, and social environments all reflect different realities and constraints. A more thoughtful and context-sensitive approach leads to more authentic districts that represent not just creative economies but creative societies.

2. **Do your homework:** ACE visionaries, builders, and managers should examine their regional arts ecology to determine whether they are better off supporting existing arts activity or building a district from scratch. Studies have shown that it is more strategic to leverage already fertile grounds rather than pursuing a top-down strategy that just shuffles arts activity to new hubs. A big part of this process is not just looking at physical places but also at uncovering the needs of the artists, creators, and makers that give districts their robustness. This initial and ongoing preparation will help ACE builders figure out if their ACE strategy, and its associated costs, can support the artists and arts activity that make the districts thrive in the short- and long-term.

3. **Connect the dots:** ACE leaders should develop integrated solutions that help build capacity. Focusing purely on arts programming and marketing keeps the district isolated in a silo, which make it difficult to achieve robust positive outcomes. Builders and managers should think about connections in the broad sense: is the district physically connected to the city's infrastructure, is the district politically connected to other citywide initiatives (whether it is livability, sustainability, or resiliency), and so on.

4. **Invest in partnerships:** ACE leaders should identify stakeholders that can bring essential political, financial, regulatory, and cultural resources and expertise. It is wise to create partnerships from a diverse set of interests—whether it is well-funded foundations, entrenched neighborhood organizations, nearby universities and colleges, invested business and community advocates,

associated public policy staffers, or others. These stakeholders will make up different partnerships, whether it is hands-on advising or hands-off programmatic investment.

5. **Be adaptive, flexible, and nimble:** Visions and plans are wonderful and help set a longer course, but they need to accommodate the realistic and day-to-day realities of building and managing arts districts. Comprehensive and ongoing SWOT (Strength, Weaknesses, Opportunity, and Threats) analyses and conversations help district stakeholders determine how to navigate sticky or difficult areas. Whether the district is a new, exciting concept or an established, maturing one, for the most part they all need to adapt to changing city priorities, new leadership, and periods of financial distress.

6. **Be thoughtful about your management structure:**
ACE should consider what financial and management model to follow in order to have a plan for financing and developing the district vision. Many arts district initiatives are underfunded. The key is not getting so lost in fundraising that the district leader or district organization experiences mission drift or is unable to divert time away from fundraising for operations. Many ways exist to finance arts districts, including local taxation powers, state tax incentives, philanthropic program investments, corporate branding, public façade improvement programs, Main Street programs, historic preservation programs, public/private partnerships, and more. Also a variety of ways exist to manage districts, whether it is through a public agency, a nonprofit organization, a collection of volunteers, a master developer, a community-based organization, a single entrepreneur, or a privatized model. It is important to consider management and financial structures in the short-term, but also how they might evolve depending upon a host of factors.

It is an exciting time for district enthusiasts who can help us see, imagine, and experience how arts, culture, and entertainment can help achieve broader community ambitions and make places more interesting.

Arts and culture is moving from the periphery of public policy conversations to the core. It is an exciting time for district enthusiasts who can help us see, imagine, and experience how arts, culture, and entertainment can help achieve broader community ambitions and make places more interesting. These districts are diversifying at a rapid speed, making it essential to figure out how we can best support them at a local, state, and federal level.

For more information on art, cultural, and entertainment districts, please visit the following resources:

Americans for the Arts National Cultural District Exchange at www.AmericansfortheArts.org/CulturalDistricts

Ashley, A.J. "Beyond the Aesthetic: The Historical Pursuit of Local Arts Economic Development." *Journal of Planning History*. 2015.

Sagalyn, L.B. and A.J. Ashley. "Cities as Entertainment Centers: Can Transformative Projects Create Place?" *disP - The Planning Review*. 2014.

Amanda J. Ashley is an assistant professor in the Community and Regional Planning Department of the School of Public Service at Boise State University. She teaches economic and community development, and her research has covered the topics of the politics of urban development and land use change, the relationship between civic engagement and planning policy, and the dynamics of communication in strategic planning and visioning.

Creating an Arts Master Plan for a Historic Millwork District

DUBUQUE, IA

SET ALONG A CURVE OF THE MISSISSIPPI RIVER, Dubuque, Iowa, a city of 60,000 people, draws tens of thousands of visitors each year, many coming to experience Dubuque's cultural and natural attractions. Once home to a vibrant economy founded on river-based manufacturing and milling, over the decades Dubuque's economy has shifted, leaving sections of the city in disrepair. The Historic Millwork District (HMD), which encompasses part of Dubuque's downtown and its surrounding neighborhoods, including the port of Dubuque, is comprised predominantly of these historic former mill buildings. In 2009, in line with its Comprehensive and Downtown Master Plans, the Dubuque City Council adopted the Historic Millwork District Master Plan in which it set out a vision for the revitalization of HMD from a vacant and underutilized neighborhood into a mixed-use one.

The 2007 Dubuque comprehensive plan detailed its vision for Dubuque's future around three categories: environmental/ecological integrity, economic prosperity, and social/cultural vibrancy. Combined, these three categories addressed 14 elements, including land use and urban design, infrastructure, cultural arts, and economic development. HMD is a keystone of the city's economic development strategy. As laid out in the HMD Master Plan, the city envisions the district becoming a creative, innovative, and sustainable place that propels Dubuque ahead of its regional competitors.

**Dubuque Symphony
Orchestra
performing in the
Historic Millwork
District.**
PHOTO BY
RONALD W. TIGGES

One strategy employed to achieve this is the establishment of a
creative community within the district to help transform it into a
place for gathering, interconnectivity, and inspiration. The city and
Dubuque Main Street/Downtown Dubuque Cultural Corridor (DMS/
DDCC), a nonprofit organization committed to the economic and
cultural development of the city's downtown area, created the Arts
in the District project to support this effort. Arts in the District works
not only to preserve the district's historic architecture but also to
redesign the buildings as spaces for visual and performing arts.

To start, the Arts in the District team brought together experts
on historic preservation, including historic rehabilitation company
Gronen Restoration, architecture firm Jeffrey Morton Associates,
and affordable arts facility development nonprofit Artspace to
make structural and architectural recommendations regarding
the adaptive reuse of the abandoned mills. Working with local
developers, three buildings in HMD were identified and redesigned
as spaces for art. Simultaneously, events were planned to
highlight the potential use of HMD spaces as a place for artists

Opening night dance performance at Voices, a repurposed warehouse.
PHOTO BY
RONALD W. TIGGES

to gather and attract a diverse, year-round audience. Types of events included festivals, installations, and exhibitions. Most events were kept free and open to the public with free shuttles running between event spaces, thanks to a collaboration with local transportation officials. This arts programming served to emphasize the city's interest and investment in broadening arts access in HMD, and improving its overall economy.

As a result of the Arts in the District project, the number of annual arts events has grown from one to four over the past few years, and two nonprofit arts organizations have chosen to locate their headquarters in the district. Additionally, the arts have influenced the neighborhoods surrounding HMD, with three street murals having been recently installed in the Washington neighborhood. Based on this current activity, an initial economic impact assessment has estimated a $47.2 million annual economic impact on Dubuque.

Can Arts Drive Rural Economic Development?

BY CHRIS BECK AND TRACY TAFT

RURAL AMERICA IS IMPERILED. The loss of traditional extraction industries, the mechanization of agricultural operations, and the consolidation of farms into national conglomerates are daunting present-day circumstances compounded by youth exodus to urban jobs, infrastructure decline, and persistent poverty.

At the same time, however, many rural towns are uniquely positioned to remake themselves. Housing is affordable. Old Main Street buildings and long-empty industrial buildings are ripe for creative reuses. And, in many cases, rural towns are the best entry points to vast swaths of nature and inspiring landscapes.

It does not take much to change the economic trajectory of a rural place. Fifty, 25, or even ten new jobs paying decent salaries can make a big difference in tipping the economic balance of a small community. To add to that, federal and state resources exist, such as U.S. Department of Agriculture's Rural Development agency, dedicated to helping rebuild rural infrastructure and implementing communities' development strategies.

The mills and mines, in most cases, are not going to reopen. The farms are not going to employ the numbers of people they used to. However, many rural towns have other assets that appeal to the next generation of Americans and even to the silver tsunami of baby boomers, be it a simultaneously peaceful and vibrant place to raise a family or an affordable community in which to retire where creative activities and people are regularly in the mix.

Children participating in the Ajo Plaza Festival in Ajo, Arizona.
PHOTO BY JEWEL CLEARWATER, ISDA

CAN ARTS AND CULTURE MAKE A SIGNIFICANT ECONOMIC DIFFERENCE IN RURAL AMERICA?

With leadership from the National Endowment for the Arts and a consortium of national philanthropies (i.e. ArtPlace America), many rural communities are exploring strategies that use arts and culture as new economic drivers to revitalize their towns.

From Haines, Alaska, to Blue River, California, and Ajo, Arizona, from Wisconsin Rapids, Wisconsin, to Wilson, North Carolina, Whitesburg, Kentucky, and Eastport, Maine—local leaders, citizens, nonprofits, community foundations, and elected officials are exploring new approaches to revitalizing their towns. Some are working to attract new artists, entrepreneurs, rural-based teleworkers, boomer retirees, and millennial "creatives." Others are identifying and building on local assets, restoring Main Street buildings and performance venues, and nurturing local theaters and homegrown bands. The challenge for leaders in this new field of creative placemaking is to combine these efforts to create economic vitality without losing local authenticity.

So, given a combination of extraordinary challenges and opportunities in rural towns, how can the arts be deployed as part of a broader economic development effort? And what are some core ingredients that make such a strategy work?

Based on what we are learning, below is an incomplete list of the types of rural creative placemaking projects that towns are testing.

- **Artist housing.** Providing affordable housing and workspace for artists, young and old, is a sure way to bring new energy to the community.
- **Artist residencies.** Establishing short- and long-term residencies is another way to attract new people to a community.
- **Pop-up businesses.** Supporting affordable incubator spaces on Main Street will give a chance for entrepreneurs to test their ideas and build new businesses.
- **Creative workforce development.** Providing new skills for workers in artisan industries, including woodwork, glass, metal, cultural tourism, creative technology, and even the construction of arts and cultural facilities.
- **Quality lodging.** Promoting bed-and-breakfasts and other lodging businesses in the heart of the community (not on the highway strip!) is an essential ingredient in any community trying to implement cultural tourism strategies.
- **Performance and festivals.** Establishing financially sustainable festivals and supporting regular and high-quality performances is important in many places.
- **Famous local people or movements.** Celebrating the achievement of former residents whose stories and work attract outside interest is another approach.
- **Connect local food to local art.** The local food movement is growing rapidly and many communities are connecting the dots between the creative people working in both fields.

Incorporating these approaches and elements into economic development work can help to attract a new generation of visitors and lead to them staying longer and returning more frequently. It also may entice new residents to plant roots. Or it may be just the ingredients necessary to re-energize local spirit and entice native sons and daughters to return after college with the confidence that their hometown has a future.

To implement culture-based rural economic strategies, we have found that a few key elements are helpful for success.

- **Leadership.** First and foremost, the community must have citizen leaders and elected officials who embrace bringing cultural strategies to the table and supporting these strategies with policy (e.g. smart zoning) and money.
- **Good bones.** Having attractive, well-constructed old buildings is often an important ingredient to rural revitalization.
- **Main Street focus.** Towns that make a strategic decision to target most public and private investments into the historic town centers have a better chance of succeeding. As populations shrink, investment and subsidy to rural highway strips further diffuses economic activity and continues a town's decline. Young people, and really all people, liked the Main Streets of old. The past is often truly the best path to a bright future.
- **Strong partnerships and inclusiveness.** Building an array of partnerships with all the people and organizations that make up the community is essential. Business leaders and commercial property owners need to embrace the strategy. All the racial and ethnic groups in rural places must believe that their voices are heard and that their aspirations are included. Towns that rely on the narrow goals and interests of a small group of even well-intentioned people will not succeed.
- **Regional collaboration.** Towns that work with other towns and counties as part of a larger geographical strategy are more likely to succeed. Rural areas are going to continue to lose population, so it will be even more important in the future to shed town and county rivalries and instead combine forces to secure resources for a truly regional approach.

Even with some or all of these ingredients, the path to a new rural economy will be bumpy. However, with committed, open-minded leaders who embrace collaboration with new people, fresh ideas, and broad-based community input—not to mention who have a lot of patience—an arts-driven economic strategy can take root and lead to very positive economic outcomes.

And here are a few examples of rural communities that are executing creative placemaking strategies to foster new vitality and promote new economic opportunity.

Ajo, Arizona. This former copper-mining town in a multi-ethnic high-poverty area near the border is harnessing its extraordinary assemblage of Spanish Revival-style buildings to form an integrated community revitalization strategy that is restoring vitality to the town center as the hub of commerce, and a regional destination for artists, performance, festivals, and more.

Southwest Virginia. This rural region on the edge of Appalachia is developing a regional economic strategy around the arts and nature-based recreation. Towns are reopening venues for performance, and businesses such as bed and breakfasts, food service, and outdoor outfitters are working to cater to tourists seeking inspiration and a refuge from the city.

Clarksdale, Mississippi. Located in the heart of one of the poorest pockets of the country along the Mississippi River, the city's local leaders decided to capitalize on their legacy as a birthplace of the nation's blues music. Their cultural tourism strategy is attracting visitors from across the globe to festivals and new entertainment venues, and restaurants are thriving now where even five years ago there seemed little hope.

Wilson, North Carolina. This once thriving tobacco mill town was home to a significant folk artist, Vollis Simpson, who for decades designed and hand-constructed hundreds of small and large metal windmills, known as "whirligigs," in his barn. Wilson is now hoping to place 30 of these windmills on what will be a new park on Main Street and that will hopefully become a regional attraction that will drive the renovation of old buildings and be available for centrally located businesses.

Wisconsin Rapids, Wisconsin. The recent closure of a large paper mill had huge negative impacts on the economic vibrancy of the city. A local community foundation purchased the vacant former headquarters of the local newspaper in the heart of downtown to help counteract this economic slump. This new community hub is intended to help attract other nearby investments and bring businesses back to downtown.

Eastern Kentucky. The heart of coal country may be facing the hardest current economic challenges of any region in the country. But local and federal leadership of all political stripes are putting their heads together to think of new approaches. In Whitesburg, Appalshop, a longtime multimedia cultural leader in Appalachia, provides media and technology training opportunities to youth as one means of economic diversification. In Hazard, a new river greenway trail in the heart of town is one piece of citizen-led revitalization efforts.

Blue River, California. Nestled along the Mad River where the Redwood Forest meets the Pacific, Blue River is home to Dell'Arte International, a theater school and professional company that has been a cultural hub for the area for 40 years. Dell'Arte recently expanded its training facilities to an old industrial site, which now also is home to a local brewery and beer garden.

Lanesboro, Minnesota. The town is executing a holistic strategy to fortify its economy by designating itself as an "Arts Campus." Virtually anything that happens in the town aims to have some connection to the arts, from galleries and restaurants on Main Street to park trails and pedestrian walkways.

York, Alabama. The small, scrappy Coleman Arts Center is leading the charge to integrate arts and commerce on the Main Street of this quiet racially diverse town in the high-poverty area of the agricultural Black Belt of the South, known for its rich black soils and productive croplands. The arts center now owns nearly ten buildings, including the local library. It hosts artist residencies, an art gallery, and is developing a pop-up business incubator on Main Street where local entrepreneurs can kick-start a business.

Eastport, Maine. Dealing with a decline in maritime industries and the realities of long, dark, cold winters and extreme remoteness—it is the easternmost point of the country—leaders in this town have embarked on an effort to restore dilapidated 19th-century buildings as temporary work/live spaces for artists and businesses. Throw in a handful of festivals and a frosty "First Night" celebration on New Year's, and who knows what sort of people will call Eastport home?

Haines, Alaska. The city sits at the foot of towering snow-capped peaks along the Pacific Ocean and the state's famous glaciers. These days, it bases its economy on the cruise ships that dock there. With a desire to make their disheveled Main Street a more appealing experience, storefronts are now sporting the work of local artists, and businesses are seeing the value of using the arts as a way to provide visitors (and local residents) with a positive experience in the town center.

All of these communities are recipients of national foundation grants and a host of other public and private investments. All of these towns also have big challenges to overcome, and economic transformation is in no way guaranteed. With strategies focusing on their Main Street neighborhoods, continued public and philanthropic investments, openness to change and innovation, tolerance of new viewpoints and diverse populations, rural communities across the country will have a better chance of creating new economic opportunities.

Chris Beck was a senior projects advisor for USDA Rural Development through spring 2016, where he provided strategic support for USDA's efforts in promoting effective community and economic development approaches in rural regions, collaborating with national and regional philanthropies to leverage greater support in rural America, and strategizing around local and regional food systems policy.

Tracy Taft served as executive director of the International Sonoran Desert Alliance (ISDA) for 13 years and continues to work as its executive advisor. Prior to working in Ajo, Arizona, with ISDA, Taft spent 15 years in Washington, DC, building the NeighborWorks Training Institute and developing the Gateway CDC in Prince George's County, Maryland.

Reimagining a Historic School and Town Center

AJO, AZ

A FORMER COPPER-MINING TOWN in the middle of the Sonoran Desert, Ajo, Arizona, is a two-hour drive southwest of Phoenix and a two-and-a-half-hour drive west of Tucson. It was originally established by John and Isabella Greenway as a company town, consisting of three separate, segregated towns in one (Indian Village, Mexican Town, and Ajo). The town's design was inspired by the City Beautiful Movement, with the town center anchored by an arcaded plaza connecting the train depot and the town's most prominent building, the Curley School. Historically, the town center was the only place where residents of all three townships mixed and enjoyed community events; outside the town center, cultural and ethnic divisions were prevalent due to institutional racism.

Today, the copper mine is gone; Indian Village and Mexican Town are no longer; and the connection between the train depot, plaza, and Curley School has deteriorated due to the decreased popularity of railroad travel. Ajo's year-round population is only 3,300 (a quarter of what it was before the mine closed). It is 10 percent Native-American and 40 percent Hispanic; and nearly a third of its residents live in poverty. Concurrently, Ajo has a significant seasonal population as many retirees have begun to purchase property in town. Despite this influx of snow birds, there is a severe lack of economic opportunity. Only half of the community's working-age adults are in the labor market at all, and nearly half of those who work have only part-time jobs.

In an effort to revive Ajo's economy, the community is trying to transform the town into a tourist destination with a focus on arts and culture. In 2007, the International Sonoran Desert Alliance (ISDA), a local nonprofit, converted the Curley School into a destination for artists from all over the country to come live and work. The campus

New design plans for the town plaza of Ajo, Arizona.
IMAGE COURTESY OF ROB PAULUS ARCHITECTS

now houses 30 affordable live/work units, artist studios, a clay shop, a wood shop, a gallery, and an international retreat center focused on cultural and eco-tourism.

Extending their work beyond the campus, ISDA—in collaboration with Pima County and key local organizations, including the public school and the Chamber of Commerce—began plans to redesign Ajo's town center, starting with the historic plaza. ISDA and Pima County selected the design team of ARC Studios—a landscape design firm—in Phoenix and Rob Paulus Architects in Tucson to develop plans for the site. They started by conducting a variety of surveys and holding multiple design charrettes, rounds of discussion, and special events.

This broad, multicultural, and multigenerational community participation informed the final design ideas, which were submitted to the public for review online and at the public library. After the review process and much discussion with ISDA and Pima County, the architects provided revised design suggestions. The final design options helped to unify the experience of the whole town center and beautify the specific areas identified by the community. Using a combination of pavers, shade trees, and bougainvillea vines in an innovative way, the designs aimed to simultaneously slow traffic, attract attention, and visually connect the plaza and the broad avenue leading to the Curley School.

Through this process, the town came to understand the importance of community dialogue, and its ties to feelings of ownership, both negative and positive. Negatively, some community residents became very angry that ISDA and the county would consider making any changes whatsoever to the historic plaza. Positively, a community group, "Friends of the Plaza," was created to maintain the plaza, complete beautification projects, and raise money for its enhancement. Construction has begun, and even though renovations are not yet complete, the redesign project is already a success as it has brought the community as a whole back to the town center, improving community relations and giving residents a "new" place to gather.

Chapter 3

community identity + belonging

Building Economy and Community with Cultural Assets

BY BEN FINK AND MIMI PICKERING

WHEN A FRIEND VISITING FROM PHILADELPHIA compared Whitesburg, Kentucky, to Stars Hollow, all she got from us was a blank stare. Turns out Stars Hollow is the setting of *Gilmore Girls*: a small idyllic town, rural and intimate, yet diverse and open-minded. When our friend arrived in Whitesburg—a former coal-mining town in one of the poorest and sickest Congressional districts in the country—she thought such a place could exist only on TV. Twenty-four hours later, she had changed her mind.

What did it? Was it coffee and breakfast at a local restaurant, whose owners routinely keep it open late for community events? Or late-night drinks at a new bar where the proprietor, a former opera singer, spent an hour discussing the finer points of vocal technique? Or the time spent browsing books and crafts at an Appalachian heritage store, enjoying music at a cooperatively owned record shop, sharing stories with locals of all ages and political stripes, or sampling homemade moonshine at a family-owned distillery?

More than anything, probably, it was the general sense that *things are happening here*. Yes, the coal industry is pulling out, and jobs are on the decline. (At last count, there are fewer than 100 coal-mining jobs left in Letcher County.) Yet young people are starting tattoo parlors and artist collectives. Senior citizens are fighting to keep their defunded community centers open. High school students and retirees alike host programs on WMMT community radio. And the independent weekly, the *Mountain Eagle*, still bears the masthead: "It Screams!" In the face of economic decline, the people of Whitesburg are building a new economy.

Pick and Bow Concert in Whitesburg, Kentucky.
PHOTO BY MIMI PICKERING

How did this happen? Ask many people around here, and they'll point you to a strange-looking building on the edge of town; painted on the walls is the name "Appalshop." Founded in 1969 as one of ten Community Film Workshops funded by the War on Poverty's Office of Economic Opportunity, Appalshop includes a filmmaking company (Appalshop Films/Headwaters Television), youth media training (Appalachian Media Institute), a theater company (Roadside Theater), a record label (June Appal Recordings), an extensive archive, and the aforementioned community radio station (WMMT) broadcasting to at least three states. Together, these projects constitute the largest body of creative works about Appalachia in the world.

What does all this have to do with building the economy? Turns out, a whole lot. From its origins as a career-training program for young Appalachians, Appalshop has always been about economic development. It creates jobs both directly, for local filmmakers, musicians, recording artists, archivists, and educators; and indirectly, through extensive partnerships with artisans, growers, chefs, tech companies, healthcare providers, school systems, and governments across the region. These partnerships are a key element in Appalshop's role as a "culture hub," a dynamic center of cross-sector cultural activity.

Yet Appalshop's biggest economic role may be in *creating the conditions* for creating jobs. A national leader in grassroots arts, Appalshop has pioneered the practice of "first voice/authentic voice," creating culture of and by the people of Appalachia, not about them. Appalshop documentaries have no narrator: every word is spoken by the people being documented. Roadside Theater plays have no script: every word comes from stories told and recorded by participants. Appalshop's administrative offices are filled with old-time musicians, radio hosts, filmmakers, visual artists, organizers, and community activists: at Appalshop there is no producers-versus-consumers, servers-versus-served, us-versus-them. There is only us, here, together, building our collective voice in a region where so many feel voiceless.

Strengthening the capacity of residents to exercise voice, agency, and ownership over their community affairs is essential to their ability to create communities that they value.

In the words of the economist Fluney Hutchinson, who has worked in developing communities all over the world: "Strengthening the capacity of residents to exercise voice, agency, and ownership over their community affairs is essential to their ability to create communities that they value...That's the kind of economic development that ensures that we all are invested and remain invested because it represents and it recognizes our unique ability to contribute to it."

Hutchinson and his institute, the Economic Empowerment and Global Learning Initiative at Lafayette College, have been working with Appalshop since 2013. Together, we are building on the Appalshop model of bottom-up, culturally based economic development, a model which may turn many more high-poverty American towns into Stars Hollow.

Ben Fink is the creative placemaking project manager at Appalshop. He has produced grassroots theater with faith, labor, and neighborhood organizations in the Twin Cities; organized and consulted with homelessness nonprofits in Connecticut; and directed youth theater, writing, and community engagement programs in rural southern New Jersey.

Mimi Pickering is the director of community media initiative at Appalshop. She is also an award-winning filmmaker whose documentaries often feature women as principal storytellers, focus on injustice and inequity, and explore the efforts of grassroots organizations to address community problems that frequently reflect global issues.

Ethics of Development:
A Shared Sense of Place

BY MARÍA LÓPEZ DE LEÓN

A SENSE OF PLACE IN LATINO/A COMMUNITIES

Arts and culture in Latino communities are a manifestation of the values, creativity, visions, and aspirations of the people who make those communities their home. Latino families—past, present, and future—simultaneously occupy physical and spiritual places that express who we are as a diverse humanity and as individuals. Very often, the physical layout of our communities is a framework for shared social and cultural activity. This layout, however, is never restricted to solely buildings, parks, centers, material neighborhoods, and so forth. It includes intangible or even temporal spaces that may be the result of cultural practices, such as the spaces in which marches, festivities, or ancestral rituals take place. These sites of spiritual and cultural meanings can even easily translate from one physical location to another.

It is through our cultural practices that we have the ability to bridge the ancient with the new in order to advance into a shared future, connecting our ancestors and elders to our youth, to our children and grandchildren. In thinking about best practices regarding the role of the arts in community development, questions arise on how to best engage Latino communities in creative placemaking work. These questions can, at times, appear to pose a one-dimensional, prescriptive answer, as if Latinos are somehow different, suggesting a tendency to stereotype those we do not know. There is nothing *different* in the way one engages Latino communities—respect and inclusion are touchstones to success in any community.

The character and texture of a community's cultural life is expressed through artmaking and is often what centers neighborhoods, allowing one to view the inseparability of the arts from education, community development, personal growth, and socio-economic equity.

***Blooming in the Midst
of Gentrification* mural
in San Francisco,
California.**
PHOTO COURTESY OF
DIGITAL MURAL PROJECT,
2014

Through models of true civic participation, creative placemaking can be approached in ways that celebrate and promote inclusion and vibrancy by way of a more collective effort, wherein the set of stakeholders consist of a whole community participating in defining and shaping the remaking of a place.

SUPPORTING ALREADY MADE SPACES

Together in community, it is possible to envision a new future and look beyond purely economic developmental gains by examining the intent to re-create a given place, considering who and what economic and social issues are there already, and then together determining how to help "revitalize" instead of replace the existing community. By leveraging the creative potential already present within a community, one can invest in and valorize the existing cultural life and offerings of residents. In other words, engaging community in respectful, inclusive civic planning processes within their homes and neighborhoods is of utmost importance in order to achieve real, long-term, sustainable outcomes that build equity and capacity within a place.

As the dialogue of creative placemaking initiatives continues to evolve in the larger context of economic and urban revitalization efforts, there is a need for places of being—that is, places primarily determined by our modes of being in them, by how we inhabit them creatively as different cultural groups—rather than places inscribed with directions on how we should inhabit them.

These places of being could also be described as places of belonging, or anchoring, and could be compared to what Dr. Karen Olwig describes in her article "Islands as Places of Being and Belonging": "Islands may be usefully conceptualized as socio-cultural constructs that constitute important anchoring points as well as sources of identification."[1] Ideally, we can say that these places of being are those anchoring sites where we can map and identify the existing ecosystems of our communities through an artistic and cultural lens. These places should embrace diverse voices and identities, including both individual and collective expression and welcoming both intergenerational and intersector dialogues. Building the connective tissue of communities promotes intersectorial work and increases access for economic advancement and revitalization based on a strategy of equity and social justice.

There is a need for places of being—that is, places primarily determined by our modes of being in them, by how we inhabit them creatively as different cultural groups.

LEARNING FROM WHAT WORKS AND WHAT DOES NOT

Fortunately, there exist today many examples of successful creative placemaking models that work with diverse communities. Across the nation, Latino community-based arts and cultural organizations, as Dr. Tomas Ybarra Frausto asserts, "[counter] the prevalent deficiency model that [reduces] Spanish-speaking communities to a set of problems with an asset-based model that [fuses] the cultural capacity and agency of the groups as springboards for self invention and self determination."

For example, in Puerto Rican neighborhoods within New York, Philadelphia, and many other locales, there exists the tradition of the Casitas. These are creative, social hubs for the performance of music, dance, and other expressions that transmit cultural knowledge to the broader city and engage participants not merely as audiences or consumers, but as interpreters of a shared experience. Creative placemaking practitioners are well-placed to strategically focus on the thousands of grassroots arts and cultural

[1]Olwig, Karen Fog. "Islands as Places of Being and Belonging." *Geographical Review*. American Geographical Society. 2007.

organizations like these in neighborhoods across the country, and invest in the growth and stabilization of "already made" creative sites and contribute to their growth and stabilization.

Unfortunately, unhealthy models of creative placemaking also exist in neighborhoods across our country, models that result in gentrification and the eventual displacement of the people who call that place home. This work often results in the disarticulation of a community's cultural practices and its replacement with a culture driven simply by financial imperatives. An example that comes to mind is the ongoing gentrification of San Francisco's Mission District, where a predominantly Latino working class is being displaced by skyrocketing rents and increased costs of housing. Many Latino artists and cultural practitioners and organizations, such as Galeria de la Raza and the Mission Cultural Center—who have lived and worked in the Mission District for decades—have been priced out of their homes and work spaces. The time has come for us to re-examine redevelopment methods that result in supplanting entire communities and find balanced approaches to building our cities and towns.

The ability to learn from these models puts us in a great position to work in true partnerships with the varied communities we serve. As part of this, it is important for us to foster equality as a key component in these partnerships. As a member of the Latino community, I think about the growing young Latino demographic that already makes up 25 percent of all U.S. schoolchildren, and consider what opportunities the future will hold for them to produce culture and integrate who they are into the larger "American" imagination. The creativity of artists transforms places and, for me, artists represent what Pope Francis calls *social poets*, "those whose energy encourages the creation of work...and gives inspiration to communities on the margins."

The time has come for us to re-examine redevelopment methods that result in supplanting entire communities and find balanced approaches to building our cities and towns.

María López De León is the executive director of the National Association of Latino Arts and Cultures and a member of the NEA's National Council on the Arts. She is also a cultural organizer and practitioner dedicated to strengthening communities through the arts and has multiple years of experience working with Latino artists and arts organizations.

Understanding Local Cultural Assets

LOS ANGELES (WILLOWBROOK), CA

FOR DECADES, OUTSIDERS DEFINED the unincorporated South Los Angeles area of Willowbrook by what it lacked. Most perceived the neighborhood and its adjacent communities of Watts and Compton as ground zero for poverty, gang violence, and low educational attainment; critical issues included socio-economic challenges, cultural division, and limited access to healthcare. However, the area has seen significant investment by the county in recent years, including the reopening of the Martin Luther King Medical Campus in 2014 after its controversial shutdown in 2007. Willowbrook has had a number of projects on the table related to enhancing infrastructure, health services, and community development. Yet even with the county supporting the area, it was not clear how Willowbrook's distinct identity would be reflected in these improvements. Planners and organizations had long focused on the community, but their plans had not always gained traction with the intended beneficiaries. The Los Angeles County Arts Commission (LACAC) developed a new arts-related asset map and visioning document that emerged from an in-depth community input process and was aimed precisely at the idea of having the community voice its own identity.

Art needed to become a vehicle for galvanizing residents and characterizing the distinct cultural identity of Willowbrook. LACAC engaged in a close conversation with the community to identify its needs and aspirations, translating these into a long-term program for the arts. LACAC tapped two key partners to implement the project: LA Commons and artist Rosten Woo. LA Commons—a Los Angeles-based nonprofit organization that facilitates and helps materialize local art practices—provided preliminary research, conducted community member interviews, and mapped the area's cultural assets. Rosten Woo was experienced with

this type of work, having co-founded the Center for Urban Pedagogy, a nonprofit organization that uses art to encourage civic participation. Woo contributed artistic vision and expertise in public engagement and urban planning. Numerous local organizations served as on-the-ground community organizers, conducting outreach, hosting focus groups, connecting the Project Willowbrook team with additional stakeholders, and giving team leaders feedback on the project. Their intensive engagement gave the project validity in the eyes of residents, which ultimately strengthened the project's content, audience, and relevance.

This project was not the first time groups had developed visions for Willowbrook; the community had developed planning fatigue and felt tired of contributing to visions that, over the course of decades, went unrealized. So for LACAC, the challenge was not only to create a visioning tool but also to develop real relationships with residents in order to overcome disillusionment with the planning process. The team split the project into two phases. For the first phase, LA Commons and LACAC did extensive interviews with community members and mapped the area's existing cultural sites and activities. This process allowed the team to understand its site and to develop relationships with key community stakeholders and residents. In Phase II, the team developed novel approaches to involving the community in communicating and developing the visioning document, culminating into *Willowbrook is/Willowbrook es...*, a magazine-like survey and visualization of the resident's talents, a community showcase, a home-and-garden tour and book, and the visioning document, all of which included the many contributions of community members themselves.

Willowbrook is/Willowbrook es... is a community-driven document meant to serve as a way to coalesce different ideas outlined by residents and as a framework for the future of Willowbrook. Furthermore, the project gave different county departments a vision around which they could develop their own strategies in a coordinated way. As Letitia Ivins, assistant director of LACAC's Civic Art Program, said, "The project strengthened the County's approach to community development by ensuring that the place-defining cultural characteristics and opportunities of Willowbrook were acknowledged, supported, and written in the blueprints of its long-term future."

The project captured the community's imagination in ways that were far more enthusiastic than previous attempts at planning Willowbrook. This positive reception was evidenced by the community holding book launch parties for Woo to celebrate the community-sourced visioning document. In fact, the creative approach to urban planning outlined in the book sufficiently impressed the Office of Supervisor Mark Ridley-Thomas of Los Angeles County enough that it requested similar approaches for five other unincorporated communities.

How Artists Share (in) Place: A Journey to Oglala Lakota Land

BY JUDILEE REED

OVER TEN YEARS, I HAVE MADE FOUR TRIPS to South Dakota, stopping first in Rapid City before traveling on to the Pine Ridge Reservation. Each time, I came at the invitation of the First Peoples Fund, a service organization supporting the development of Native-American artists and culture-bearers through direct financial support, infrastructure development, and training programs.

On this occasion, I traveled with a large group of foundation professionals, board members, an elected official, artists, and community leaders. Each of us had a slightly different relationship to the Native-American communities we were visiting and we all viewed this trip as an opportunity to learn more about the context in which investments of time, money, and other resources were improving the lives of people.

VISITING PINE RIDGE RESERVATION

Our journey first took us three hours north and east to the Cheyenne River Indian Reservation where we met with organizations working to provide financial services to artists and creative businesses, ranchers who were breaking down barriers to personal development with skill- and confidence-building horsemanship, and a youth center engaging young people with mural painting as a form of self-expression to stave off other threats like truancy and drugs. Our day was packed with inspiring stories told across many miles of rural country.

Over the course of the first day, I thought about the maps I consulted prior to my trip, and how abstract the Badlands National Park and the southwest piece of the state carved out as the Pine Ridge Reservation are as drawings describing land designations.

It is the quality of crisp air and clear light, long distances of travel between one destination to the next, and, most of all, the stories told by our guides—artists and community leaders—that create understanding of the land and the culture of the Lakota people.

On the morning of the second day, we awoke in the land of Oglala Lakota people. A small group of us woke early for a meeting with businessman and First Peoples Fund artist Guss Yellow Hair (Lakota) who played his drum and offered a morning prayer. As he played, the work and the expressions of optimism, perseverance, and resilience we had heard about the day before came into sharp focus set against the ancient ragged shapes of Badlands that is at once haunting and majestic. What so often felt bifurcated and illogical—the deep challenges the people were addressing and the breathtaking beauty of the landscape—coexisted through Guss Yellow Hair. Through music, he connected the modern and the ancient, the transient and the timeless, creating an understanding of the land and the culture of the Lakota people through story.

In July 2015, Lakota teenager Elizabeth Eagle demonstrated fancy shawl dancing during the Cheyenne River Youth Project's inaugural RedCan graffiti jam at the innovative Waniyetu Wowapi (Winter Count) Art Park on South Dakota's Cheyenne River Sioux Reservation.
PHOTO BY RICHARD STEINBERGER COURTESY OF THE CHEYENNE RIVER YOUTH PROJECT

CHANGING THE STORY FOR THE LAKOTA PEOPLE

Two centuries of task force reporting and federal data describe poverty, high levels of alcohol and drug addiction, high suicide rates, failed health and education support, and discrimination. However, this trip offered a different perspective on the same story. A series of reflections demonstrated the resilience and ingenuity of their collective efforts to improve the lives of the Lakota people. At the Thunder Valley Community Development Corporation, we learned of leader Nick Tilsen's support of young people and their families in ways that reconnect them with their traditional Lakota culture and help them navigate pathways out of poverty and toward sustainable lives. Later, teens from Red Cloud Indian School who participated in the First Peoples Fund's Youth Speaks Dances with Words poetry and spoken word program shared beautiful poems of mourning and of pride. As the poets took the stage, outside clouds formed and lightning shot through the sky—once again, reminding us of the interconnection of the people, the art and culture, and the landscape.

I was reminded of the myriad ways artists connect us to places and that places connect us to the expressions of artists, and how these things combined elevate our sense of both in ways that we only barely understand.

ART AND CULTURE ARE INSEPARABLE FROM LIFE

On the rare occasions that the value of art and culture is accounted for in the Lakota culture, it is presented as surplus to the other things that are understood as core necessities. However, what artists and leaders who understand Pine Ridge will attest is that art and culture are core and integrated with the other dimensions of health, sustainability, and vitality that people seek.

Sculptor Brendon Albers (Minnieconjou) described this integration elegantly with the collection of stories he shared with me and fellow diners on the first night of our trip. He talked about his stone sculptures and how they enter the market through galleries, his carved pipes and other pieces that never enter a commercial market but are held by elders, used in ceremony, and are gifted to family and friends. He creates art as a means of cultural practice as well as a means of financial support. While the barriers to accessing markets to sell his sculptures may at first seem high—in this vast, empty landscape, he described a lively ecosystem that is predominantly regional in scale and that he is working to expand nationally through online sales with a gallery on the East Coast.

In the coming months, Brendon will embark on a creative placemaking venture called Rolling Rez Arts (See Lori Pourier's article in this publication). This art workshop and credit union office is a refurbished van that will bring Brendon (among a small group of select artists, including painter Don Montileaux) to share both his cultural knowledge and his practice as a working artist to young people through Pine Ridge. Here again, the complex picture connecting the traditional with the modern is affirmed.

LESSONS FOR ALL OF US

Traveling over two days across South Dakota, moving from north to south and back again, listening to stories from people whose families have lived here for generations, was a real-time lesson about Native-American people and culture that have survived through the often forced embrace of both traditional practice and modern systems of living for survival. What was so striking on my return to this special place was the multigenerational expression of perseverance and commitment to solving problems and addressing the complexity of dual citizenship of a First Nation and the United States of America with a forward-thinking sense of purpose and ingenuity.

Art and culture are core and integrated with the other dimensions of health, sustainability, and vitality that people seek.

With each story, the challenges born from hundreds of years of struggles under layers of failed U.S. policies found a counterpoint of peace and resilience in traditional practice, the strength of family and community, and the art and culture that reflects the complex ethnic identity of indigenous people. Across our brief time, I was reminded of the myriad ways artists connect us to places and that places connect us to the expressions of artists, and how these things combined elevate our sense of both in ways that we only barely understand. Communities throughout the United States have much to learn from the Lakota experience.

Judilee Reed is the director of the Thriving Cultures Program at the Surdna Foundation. Reed's career in arts and culture focuses on artists, communities, and the systems that support them. Her work spans more than two decades and includes roles at local, regional, and national scales in governmental and private organizations.

Art: A Way of Life in Native Communities

BY LORI POURIER

Ben Black Elk with pipe at altar.

THERE IS NO WORD FOR ART IN LAKOTA. We cannot separate art from how we live. Perhaps the closest concept is *wolakota*, "in peace" or "a way of life." It is how we acknowledge each other and creation as relatives. It is how we help each other and contribute to the Collective Spirit. It is our cultural way of life that we, as Native people, strive to hold onto for sustenance. Art grounds us and exemplifies who we are. Art is wolakota and central to our way of walking and living in the world.

Wolakota embodies our core values of *yuonihan* (honor), *ohola* (respect), *owothanla* (integrity) and *wounsiic' iye* (humility), which guide us in our relationship to our community, land, and place. Indigenous peoples on this continent cannot separate art from land from who we are. Lakota creation stories and our tribal teachings tell us how we came to be on this earth, that we are relatives of creation itself. Place is another of our most essential and powerful relatives.

OUR PLACE OF ORIGIN

The *Lakota Oyate* creation story tells us that we emerged from present day Wind Cave National Park located in southwestern South Dakota, near our sacred *He Sapa* (Black Hills). Here we first surfaced as human beings (the two-legged) and met our relatives, the buffalo nation. Located in and around He Sapa are five historic sites that remain sacred places to the Lakota. Most significant is *Ki iyanka Ocanku*, the sacred circle or race track, which circles the Black Hills where the people followed the sun path from spring equinox to summer solstice. *Paha Sapa* (Black Butte), *Mato Tipi* (Bear Lodge) or known today as Devil's Tower, *Mato Paha* (Bear Butte), and *Mnikata* (Hot Springs), along with the lands encompassed in our present-day reservation boundaries, define place for Lakota people.

Our Lakota ancestors valued and understood their relationship to *Unci Maka* (Grandmother Earth) and their responsibility to care for her. Sadly, as I reflect on wolakota, our peaceful way of life, it is a struggle to uphold in our contemporary environment. The way of life that our grandparents understood so well was taken from the generations that followed, disrupting the very roots of our tribal identity and culture. Federal policies and legislation, such as the General Allotment Act of 1887 (The Dawes Act), Indian Reorganization Act 1934, Indian Termination Act (1953 –1968), Indian Relocation Act (1953), as well as the lack of federal recognition and respect of our sacred ceremonial gathering places, disrupted our access and relationship to place and contributed to the deterioration of wolakota.

Looking at my family's story, by the late 1800s, when the Lakota were no longer permitted to freely move throughout their ancestral homelands, the government having removed them from He Sapa to the Red Cloud Agency (present day Pine Ridge Reservation), my grandmother Olivia Black Elk Pourier's grandfather, the famed Nicholas Black Elk (1863–1950), traveled with Buffalo Bill's Wild West show. The same regalia that he once proudly wore alongside other chiefs of our tribe was relegated to a performance regalia. After leaving Buffalo Bill's show in the late 1920s, he became part of a pageant at the site that would soon become Mount Rushmore. For the remainder of his life, he and his *tiwahe* (family) spent summer months as part of the pageant educating tourists about Lakota heritage, in the same place as his ancestors once summered. This family tradition continued through the 1950s with my great-grandfather Ben Black Elk, my grandmother Olivia Black Elk Pourier, and the rest of the Black Elk family.

My story and my work reflect the lives of many generations of Oglala Lakota that came before me—those who understood freedom on their lands, those struggling to communicate and share our history, and those like my grandmother who fought for economic opportunity through our culture and art.

NEW WAYS OF CREATIVITY & RESILIENCY

Although so much has been taken from us as Native peoples, we are still creative, resilient, and innovative. We continue to innovate wolakota. In fall 2015, Rolling Rez Arts, a mobile unit that will serve as a classroom for emerging artists, youth poets, young filmmakers, and culture bearers who want to pass on their knowledge to the next generation, was unveiled. Through this mobile unit, First Peoples Fund-certified artist-success coaches and Lakota Fund business coaches will offer values-based professional development and marketing workshops across nine districts on the Pine Ridge Reservation (roughly the size of the State of Connecticut)[1].

Built on cross-sector collaboration between the First Peoples Fund, Lakota Funds, and Artspace Projects, Rolling Rez Arts is an artist-led model of economic development and social equity for artist and culture bearers. Launched with support from the Bush Foundation's Community Innovation Award and Artplace America, in addition to the workshops, the program will provide artist mentoring and teaching and financial education and banking services through the Lakota Federal Credit Union.

Over the last 16 years, First Peoples Fund has come to recognize that we are not successful unless we help artists and the systems that support them. We believe artists are stronger when they celebrate their own resilience and vitality and begin to envision a hopeful future, and even re-imagine a new and equitable *wolakokiciyapi* (way of life in community).

> **We are not successful unless we help artists and the systems that support them. We believe artists are stronger when they celebrate their own resilience and vitality and begin to envision a hopeful future.**

None of this work is possible in isolation. Just as my current role as president of First Peoples Fund would not have been personally possible had it not been for my elders' leadership and journey, the innovation of the Rolling Rez Arts mobile unit would not be possible without these partners. Together, we are working to improve wolakokiciyapi and practice wolakota. We bring others up with us. We acknowledge those whose shoulders we stand on. We help each other. We practice being a good relative.

[1] Fifty-one percent of Native households on Pine Ridge Reservation depend on home-based enterprises for cash income. Of the 51 percent, 79 percent consist of some form of traditional arts.

Lori Pourier's grandmother, Olivia Black Elk Pourier.
PHOTO BY RONNIE FARLEY

From a Native perspective, this is vital in the field of arts and culture. With no separation between a way of life and art, then the *only* way to do the work is collectively. How we approach the work is in fact more important than what we do.

When we unveiled the Rolling Rez Arts mobile unit, I was humbled to see this collective vision manifested in a physical form that will reach so many. Looking around the circle, just off our sacred prairies, I saw all the hands that worked to make this moment possible. Together we are wolakokiciyapi. Together we must practice a way of life in community. For our people in celebration of place, this is art and culture.

Lori Lea Pourier is president of First Peoples Fund and an enrolled member of the Oglala Lakota Nation. Through her work, Pourier has helped to turn the artistic endeavors of indigenous women into viable livelihoods and lifted the veil of invisibility that has shrouded their lives. This work has reverberated throughout Indian Country and continues to create profound, positive impacts for rural Native women and their families and communities.

Celebrating Community Identity

OLYMPIA, WA

Artist Kurt Poste during an event when Squaxin Island tribal members take the floor to welcome visitors to the week of protocol for canoe journeys.
PHOTO BY
TOM MCCULLOUGH

THE SQUAXIN ISLAND TRIBE IS A SMALL, 400-member tribe with roots on a forested island in Puget Sound. Historically, the relationship of Puget Sound tribes to non-Native populations has been contentious; as the Pacific Northwest became settled, many tribes lost land, language, and cultural practices as a result of federal policies of assimilation and relocation. Traditional methods of economic self-reliance were further impacted by the imposition of the reservation system, which curtailed their ability to hunt, fish, gather, and harvest. Because of the economic and cultural challenges the tribe faces, they continually search across the region for opportunities to celebrate and continue their own traditions while increasing understanding of their cultures by non-Native populations.

Each year, the Native-American tribes of the Pacific Northwest and the First Nation tribes of Western Canada undertake a Tribal Canoe Journey in which each tribe paddles from across the region to a specified location that changes annually. Likened to the Olympics, the event brings together an array of cultures—and more than 100 canoes. In 2012, the landing events were hosted by the Squaxin Island Tribe who chose a waterfront site in Olympia, Washington, for the final ceremonial stop. As canoes traced their way down the Puget Sound, each canoe stopped at Squaxin Island—a small, uninhabited island of just over two square miles belonging to the tribe—before their final landing. The Tribal Canoe Journey seemed like an opportunity to serve the tribe's cultural goals, while at the same time helping the Squaxin Island artisans find ways to access broader markets. The Squaxin Museum and the Longhouse Education and Cultural Center (of Evergreen State College) came together to assist the tribe with a project that would help focus on arts and culture as the center of their expression of tribal identity.

Their collective vision was to create residencies and workshops that would bring the significance of their traditional practices to the attention of broad audiences through their dances, songs, and gift-giving.

One of the central components of the canoe landing is a "potlatch" ceremony, during which the Squaxin Island Tribe would offer gifts to other participants. The tribe was determined to offer traditionally made artifacts—not store-bought souvenirs—so the Squaxin Island Museum created 15 separate eight-month art residencies plus numerous community workshops. These residencies not only produced the gifts themselves, but also created an invaluable educational experience and—most importantly—became a way to continue traditional arts practices. Some residencies also aimed to create large-scale installations that would become landscape elements throughout the community during the festivities.

More than 10,000 members of the public attended the events, participated in workshops, watched the canoe landing, and attended performances. The initiative implemented 15 major art residencies, giving artists an opportunity to practice and develop indigenous arts. These artists ranged in age from 10 to 70+ years old and represented 11 tribal groups, including Squaxin. The range of artworks included woven baskets, twined tunics, elk hide painted drums, and painted canoe paddles. Many participating artists were able to elevate their craft, opening new opportunities for exhibition and entrepreneurship. Also, the event created valuable opportunities for diverse populations to come together in a common celebration, learning about the Squaxin Island Tribal culture. Traditional arts were exhibited throughout the community, giving the public ample opportunity to closely interact with these objects.

The degree of interest that the younger generation of Squaxin Island Tribe members had in pursuing traditional arts was more enthusiastic than many had anticipated. As Tina M. Kuckkahn-Miller, director of the Longhouse Education & Cultural Center reported, "We were amazed to see how many Squaxin Island Tribal members filled the arena with dancers, drummers, and singers during the protocol ceremonies. The tribe expressed their cultural identity in so many beautiful ways—in the regalia they made, the art that was gifted to thousands of participants, and the many community members of all ages that filled the ceremonial protocol stage. People are still talking about how well they represented themselves as hosts of the 2012 Tribal Canoe Journey."

Administratively, the museum hit some unexpected benchmarks, too. An annual auction at the Squaxin Island Museum saw its attendance set a record high, increasing over 16 percent from the previous year. Based on the community interest in Squaxin Island Tribal art, the Port of Olympia is now planning a walking trail that connects installations of this indigenous art.

Chapter 4

artists + government

How Can a Planning Authority Work with an Artist to Improve Public Health Outcomes for Residents?

BY NICOLE CRUTCHFIELD

A PLANNING AUTHORITY CAN LEARN about the community it serves by working with an artist to facilitate conversation, build relationships, and define a healthy community. The City of Fargo, North Dakota, approaches city planning by working with artists in unique ways to build more healthy relationships with and learn more deeply about the community it serves. While Fargo's Planning and Development department has historically approached public health through partnerships with our public health agencies providing physical and medical treatments, we recently expanded our vision to include more passive approaches, such as exposure to nature and creating outdoor environments defined by community residents to enhance their sense of belonging and welcoming.

This broadening of the approach came about through many intimate community conversations facilitated by Jackie Brookner, the late ecological artist and primary artist on the Fargo Project. The Fargo Project was a collaboration between the city planning office and the artist to create a pilot program to transform an existing concrete storm water pond that was built in response to the disastrous flooding of the Red River in 2002, tearing apart a low-income neighborhood. The artist and myself, a planner in the city planning office, teamed with active citizens to create a community-driven design to reimagine the basin as "World Garden Commons," a multi-use space celebrating Fargo's diversity but that can still hold storm water.

Resident design engagement in Fargo, North Dakota.
PHOTO COURTESY OF THE FARGO PROJECT

Brookner was able to build a community of interest around the project by listening firsthand to the wants and needs of engaged Fargo residents. Over the course of time, Brookner, working with the City, was able to find connections between their varied needs and develop the new shared community space. As a governing agency, we learned much more about our own needs by working with Brookner than if we had worked independently.

WHY AN ARTIST MATTERED TO A PLANNING OFFICE
As a local government planning authority, our agency focuses on due process and fairness as we build and enhance our city. Our social connections to the community can fall to a lesser priority than the building of the physical city. In addition, the agency can become burdened by too much structure, hindering creativity. As an artist, Brookner helped break down these stereotypes and approached problems in a more creative way outside of the governance structure, empowering local agents of change and striking a balance between government structure and community-led initiatives.

Brookner led a team of local artists in activities that engaged residents and businesses in order to gain a deep understanding of the social culture of the neighborhoods in which the project took place. The project processes and its framework were the artists' greatest contribution to the community. Two years of artist-led conversations aided the governing authority to develop a deeper and truer understanding of community needs.

We were able to learn, observe, and translate the true barriers to underserved populations. In doing so, we uncovered the essence of our local culture, which helped define a site design and project that celebrate our unique characteristics with respectful and sensitive methods, in addition to also defining an infrastructure project. As a result, World Garden Commons touches every person in an individual way but holistically serves the city as a whole.

By letting the artist create a holistic process that touched all aspects of our city, we were able to connect more personally to the community beyond our roles as government officials.

Brookner's approach taught us that:

- In community planning, it is important to focus on relationships first, and outcomes second;
- As an agency, we need to establish the necessary time to allow for the appropriate duration of the project in order for it to breathe and for the community to find its voice and define its solutions;
- Flexibility is crucial as each project has its own timeline; every day we learned new caveats and complexities within the structure of our community; and
- Working with an artist early, prior to problem identification and definition, led to a more dynamic project.

WHAT WE PLANNED TOGETHER

The overarching principle defining the Fargo Project: World Garden Commons is to align ecology and social engagement as priorities for a healthier community. Specific project outcomes include:

- Aid for refugees recovering from trauma and homesickness;
- Job training program for an unmet native plant trade;
- Areas for residents to enjoy nature and connect with the local ecology;
- Organizational succession planning for nonprofits;

- A community garden (the first on public land in Fargo) established by area organizations;
- Representation of different cultures and celebration of differences;
- Empowerment of community voices to define and own public places and create meaning;
- Culture of belonging and welcoming;
- Passive recreation as an important community value; and
- Use of ecological principles for better land management unique to this climate.

WHAT WE LEARNED TOGETHER

Through the project, we learned that artists can break down barriers and silos—coming to a meeting with an artist as facilitator allowed people to drop their guard and be more open to creativity. With the artist approaching conversations in unexpected ways, partners were more apt to try something new and experiment and work with the Fargo Project team. As a result, many participants learned new things about themselves and the community they serve while also forming a special connection to the project; this level of involvement led to a large pool of organizational partners. Fargo city government leaders also had experiences that connected them personally to the community beyond their government role.

Overall, involvement in the Fargo Project reminded us how social engagement combined with artists as facilitators and leaders can create healthy and resilient communities. By letting the artist create a holistic process that touched all aspects of our city, we were able to connect more personally to the community beyond our roles as government officials.

Nicole Crutchfield is the planning administrator for the City of Fargo, North Dakota. Her specialties include land use planning, parks and recreation, urban design, and development. She is a licensed landscape architect and certified city planner, and serves as project manager of the Fargo Project.

Connecting Public Art, Fitness, and Storm Water Management

CHATTANOOGA, TN

Residents using the Main Terrain Art Park.
PHOTO COURTESY OF CITY OF CHATTANOOGA, ECONOMIC AND COMMUNITY DEVELOPMENT

CHATTANOOGA, TENNESSEE'S fourth-largest city, is positioned along the banks of the Tennessee River on the state's southern border with Georgia. A horseshoe bend in the river cradles the city's central area, including its downtown, the University of Tennessee at Chattanooga campus, and a post-industrial stretch known as the Southside. The Southside is bound by Interstate 24, a state highway, and the railroad, and is bisected by Chattanooga's Main Street, making it an integral part of the urban fabric. The area consists of the neighborhoods Cowart, Fort Negley, and Jefferson Heights; a low-income, affordable housing development College Hill Courts; an inner-city elementary school Battle Academy; and local businesses that employ more than 5,000 employees daily. Historically, Chattanooga was a significant contributor to the 19th-century industrial economy. With its decline, industrial tenants and jobs moved out of the Southside, leaving buildings abandoned, lots vacant, and local businesses struggling. Adding to its troubles, the area has long been prone to flooding as a result of its proximity to the river and poor storm water management. Excess rain water during heavy storms quickly pools and has little chance of being absorbed into the ground, due to both the area's swaths of impermeable asphalt and concrete and steep slopes from transportation infrastructure.

With a desire to beautify this central location and assist storm water management, the city set out to transform an unused, city-owned 1.72-acre parcel along Main Street into an activity-rich public park. Public Art Chattanooga, the Lyndhurst Foundation, and Arts Build (formerly Allied Arts for Greater Chattanooga) came together with the mayor's office, key city staff, storm water engineers, landscape architects from Ross/Fowler Landscape Architecture, artists, and a planning consultant (Kennedy, Coulter,

Rushing and Watson) to think about how best to revitalize this parcel. They decided that they wanted the site to be a civic place for nearby residents, businesses, and college students to gather and a catalyst for social and economic improvements.

Through a participatory process involving stakeholders, they clarified the project objectives, created a strategic framework, and established a timeline. As part of this and in line with Chattanooga's established public health goals, the city decided to build a park that would promote a more active, healthier lifestyle. The plan was solidified when PlayCore, a local company that manufactures outdoor recreational and fitness equipment, joined the partnership, working with the design team to provide safety compliance and recreational amenities throughout the park.

The finished Main Terrain Art Park includes public art, underground detention ponds, an oval track, and PlayCore fitness equipment. The public art consists of nine sculptures created by sculptor Thomas Sayre/Clearscapes, who was selected out of more than 60 applicants. Three of the nine pieces mimic a nearby iconic bridge. They are equipped with a wheel mounted to the base that users can turn to make the elements atop rotate. Sayre came up with the design after gathering input from local stakeholders and fitness advocates in targeted small-group sessions. The on-site detention ponds keep 1.5 million gallons of water from rushing into the city's sewer system each year; that water is then reused to irrigate the park. The running track circles the park perimeter and is divided into 50-meter segments that are marked by terrazzo inlay with text that creates four Haiku poems meant to inspire reflection among park visitors.

Since its opening in 2013, the park has become an actively used open space, a meeting space for workout groups, runners, and people moving about the city; it is no longer an area avoided by residents. Playcore has launched a line of adult fitness equipment based on the model it established for the park. And, nearby businesses and housing units are undertaking improvements on their own properties.

Top Five Lessons for Better Government Artist Residencies

BY JULIE S. BURROS AND KARIN GOODFELLOW

BOSTON AIR (ARTIST-IN-RESIDENCE) is the City of Boston's residency program. Mayor Marty Walsh envisioned Boston AIR as an opportunity to integrate artists into the development and implementation of government practices and policies. The hope was that artists could bring about transformational change to agencies ripe for re-invention. The name AIR not only stands for Artist-In-Residence, but also refers to the "breath of fresh air" that a new perspective might bring to persistent civic challenges. It also reflects the aspiration of arts leadership in Boston: that working with artists within city government would soon be "as common as the air we breathe."

FIND GREAT PARTNERS

Strong, local, trusted partners were essential to the success of our project. Massachusetts College of Art and Design, who helped us design and carry out training sessions as well the final residency jury, was the logical partner for several reasons. We had a long history of collaboration and were starting from a place of trust, and key staff members were part of our Boston Art Commission for many years. As the major public university art school in Boston and the only free-standing public college of art and design in the country, they also brought deep ties to our local artist population. Their artist-centric approach to the work was a great complement to our own civic agency expertise. New Urban Mechanics were another valued, trusted, logical partner in our efforts. This is a dynamic group of "civic innovators" embedded within the mayor's office. If any city agency wants to do something innovative, the Mechanics are a resource to them and were right by our side through the entire process.

Youth engaging in the public art project Water Graffiti for Peace as a part of the Boston Artist-in-Residence program.
PHOTO COURTESY OF THE ARTIST, SHAW PONG LIU

ADOPT AN "OPT-IN" APPROACH

Many people will wonder how you even get city agencies to agree to an artist residency program, and I strongly recommend that you ask potential agency partners to "raise their hand" and opt-in to the program. You want to work with willing partners, not agencies who feel like they are being forced to collaborate. For our pilot, it was important to have people truly show up and stick with the program for the duration. Unfortunately, this eliminated some compelling agencies that simply did not have the bandwidth or space to participate. Disappointing, but in the end, better for the program. We were upfront about the time commitment from the agency liaison, as well as the need to have an actual desk or cube for the artist—we were literal about them being "in residence." It is also possible that those who did not opt-in did not yet understand how an artist might bring transformational change to their agency. In this way, the artist residencies are helping us to share Mayor Walsh's vision to integrate the arts in all city services through genuine collaboration with our colleagues.

STAY FLEXIBLE

Be flexible. As the project evolved, we had a few curveballs thrown at us, and always tried to stay focused. For example, while forming a jury, one prospective juror said no thanks; they wanted to apply to be an artist. It was a great compliment to the program, and ultimately this artist became a valued member of our first cohort. We had the budget for ten artists in the cohort, but the jury felt very strongly about 11, so we went for it. As it happens, one of the artists dropped out, and we ended up with our intended ten, so it all worked out. We had planned on several public lectures with artists who were on the vanguard of social and civic practice; however, both time and funding ran short and we were only able to produce one public lecture.

BE INCLUSIVE

We needed to take time to allow participants to build trust, understand each other's work, and explore ideas with each other.

Since Boston AIR was a pilot, we wanted to share with the public what it was we were trying to do by having artists-in-residence in city agencies. At the start of the program, we had an open call to select our original artist cohort. More than 110 artists applied for ten slots, so we felt that we reached a very wide net of applicants. We also had originally aimed for ten city agencies and 12 participated. Some were not likely to be able to host a residency, but it helped to have them in the conversation. We also found that the joint cohort of city agency liaisons and artists needed time together. We needed to take time to allow participants to build trust, understand each other's work, and explore ideas with each other. We invited all the artists to pursue a day to shadow the city liaisons. The city agencies that made themselves the most available to the artists ended up with the most number of residencies proposed for their agencies. Finally, we held a large public presentation of the ten proposed residencies, and it garnered a lot of press and community attention. We also made sure to share on our website information about all the artists in the cohort, as well as their full proposals and an invitation to share comments with the selection committee.

AIM HIGH

Our pilot for Boston AIR would not have been the same without certain city agencies. We all felt very strongly that since police relations with community members is a topical and important issue, that they should be part of the city agency cohort. Ultimately, they were enthusiastic participants, so much so that more artists proposed residencies with Boston Police than any other agency. We also made sure to pay artists fairly for their time. It was important to us to set a precedent in this way. Fair payment also ensured that we had incredible artists applying and ultimately participating in the project.

Although still in the middle of its pilot phase, the first round of Boston AIR has garnered so much attention and support that Mayor Walsh has committed funding for a second round that will be focused on the Boston Centers for Youth and Family. This time we will have the funding for ten full residencies and can incorporate many lessons from our first foray. The timing of the launch of round two will be just after the release of the Boston Creates cultural plan. A key goal of the plan is to "integrate arts and culture into all aspects of civic life, inspiring all Bostonians to value, practice, and reap the benefits of creativity in their individual lives and in their communities," and Boston AIR is one of first ways we are moving forward with this work.

We also made sure to pay artists fairly for their time. It was important to us to set a precedent in this way.

Julie S. Burros is the chief of arts and culture for the City of Boston, and she has a strong background in fusing planning, culture, and community development together. Prior to her work in Boston, she served as the director of cultural planning at Chicago's Department of Cultural Affairs and Special Events. In that role, she was instrumental in developing the 2012 Chicago Cultural Plan, and engaging the public in the process.

Karin Goodfellow is director of the Boston Art Commission. She has a background in project management, community outreach, museum education, and visual arts, and is committed to developing accessible art resources for local communities through creative problem-solving in policy development and operations management in city and state government.

People-Centered Policing Through the Arts

BY MARTY POTTENGER

Police Chief Joe Loughlin in Portland, Maine, reviewing officers' poems and photographs.
PHOTO BY MARTY POTTENGER

AS SOCIETY RE-ENGAGES IN ADDRESSING issues that have long stymied social progress, there is a different role for art, a type of creative placemaking that puts people at the center. The process of making art dramatically increases our ability to tap into a flexible intelligence, function collaboratively, analyze complex challenges, integrate contradictory perspectives, envision a positive outcome, and take the inspired risks that lead to innovative solutions.

For the last eight years, I have explored whether arts projects can deliver solutions to problems that have everything to do with relationships and nothing to do with the arts. As director of Art At Work, on the staff of the City of Portland, Maine, I have had the honor of working with hundreds of amazing local artists, municipal employees, elected officials, and residents. Together they have created more than 500 original works and engaged tens of thousands of Mainers.

THIN BLUE LINES: POLICE + HISTORIC LOW MORALE = POETRY

My arrival happened to coincide with a crisis in the police department. The city was about to appoint a new police chief and the officers were fiercely opposed. While I had not planned for Art At Work's first project to be so challenging, reality intervened. With little positive experience with police to build on, I spent the first six months getting to know their culture—asking officers and command and administrative staff what mattered, who did they "look to" and what art—if any—was already being made? Every officer I spoke with (over 40 percent of the department) said they—and the department as a whole—were experiencing "historically low morale," a situation that any city leader or socially vulnerable resident would confirm is an expensive and potentially explosive problem to have.

Recognizing the tension between the value of collective knowledge and officers' "sealed lips" approach to their work, I strategized ideas. We needed a project where officers could explore their personal and work lives as deeply as they chose, but was also user-friendly enough to facilitate sharing with other officers as well as the public. As time went by, the connections between police work and poetry stood out to me even though the officers were quite opposed to the idea of writing poetry. Yet poetry requires a flexibility, discipline, intuition, observational capacity, edge, and muscle that uniquely reflects the work of policing. Making little headway, I made a chapbook using work from veteran soldier Brian Turner and other warrior poets, reading a few poems and handing out copies during roll call. I also looked for a companion artistic discipline that would give some officers an easier path to agreeing to join the project. Photography offered a less intense but still powerful experience so I designed a project that included both.

Working with real people and in real time offered challenges as deep as the rewards. A beloved officer, Rob Johnsey, died at home late one night, cleaning his gun, just as the poetry project was getting underway. At his memorial service, his wife asked his best friend, a lieutenant, to read one of Rob's poems. As the lieutenant began reading, he shared how shocked he was to learn that Rob wrote poetry. It was then I realized that the project, already intended to raise morale, should also raise money for Rob's widow and children. So Thin Blue Lines began—a two-year project where 40 officers, captains, lieutenants, and two police chiefs were partnered with 20 poets and 20 photographers to create two professional calendars that could be used by officers' families as well as residents to raise officers' morale on the job and at home and improve community relations by raising awareness and expectations all round.

IMPACT OF THIN BLUE LINES

Two years later, 25 percent of the city's police force had either written poems or taken photographs for two calendars that sold several thousand copies in bookstores and on Amazon.com. A W.K. Kellogg Foundation-funded evaluation showed that 83 percent of the participating officers reported that the project had significantly improved their morale. Officer Alisa Poisson's poem below represents a small yet significant outcome to Portland's officers. Not long after it was published in the first police poetry calendar, a long-contested policy that officers had to wear their hats at all times, was changed. Officers spoke openly of this being a result of the poetry calendar.

> *I Do Hate the Hat*
> *Talking to a child*
> *or a victim, someone harmed,*
> *I take it off.*

After publication, the relationship between the residents who had heard of or purchased a calendar and the police was unlike anything anyone had seen before. Three months after publishing the calendar, we hosted a police poetry reading at our main library. There the police and poets read their poems to a standing-room-only crowd. The poets all remarked that they had never been listened to that closely before. One reflected whether the poet-officers' holstered guns might have made the difference. After the reading, the audience divided up into multiple civic dialogues groups to discuss police-community relationships, each group facilitated by a different poet/officer pair. To this day, eight years later, residents still mention what an impact Thin Blue Lines had on raising their understanding and expectations of real relationships with Portland police officers. The project continued to grow over time with even more unexpected results including performances after a fatal police shooting that built relationships between outraged youth and police officers.

LESSONS LEARNED FROM THIN BLUE LINES

Building relationships, identifying and recruiting on-the-ground leaders, learning the culture(s)
Every municipal department has its own culture and way of doing things. Taking the time to learn the norms and practices of those cultures is invaluable to selecting art forms, project design, implementation, and evaluation. Leaders do not always hold official leadership positions—they include the people others go to when they need a hand. The support of both formal and informal leaders is critical for such an unusual idea—putting art to work to tackle non-arts—often "people-based"—issues.

Recognizing the police department's strong partner culture, Thin Blue Lines was designed as paired partnerships between each participating officer and a poet/photographer. It is also a culture where "showing up" is important, so participating artists were kept informed about police-related public events, whether it was Officer Johnsey's memorial, an annual awards ceremony, or the dedication of a plaque honoring those killed in the line of duty.

Listening as the primary tool in outreach, recruitment, assessment, and evaluation

Art At Work incorporates intentional listening into every activity. Incorporating "listening exchanges" establishes a welcoming and inclusive environment, decreases the number of distracting interpersonal dynamics, encourages greater diversity of participants and perspectives, and builds collaborative capacity.

Keeping the "art bar" high for the officers as well as their partner poets is a sign of respect, the kind of respect and expectation that turns historically low morale into durable pride.

Artists participating in Thin Blue Lines attended several "listening exchange" training workshops prior to meeting officers. Once the project was underway, we met regularly to share experiences, ask questions, and identify opportunities. City participants also exchanged listening to build relationships, sharpen leadership skills, and evaluate the project and process.

The surprising and critical value of enlisting stakeholders in the evaluation design process

An evaluation Field Lab organized by Animating Democracy, a program of Americans for the Arts, brought Chris Dwyer, a national evaluation expert, to the project. Her process for designing project-specific evaluations included meeting with all stakeholders to identify desirable goals and outcomes and creation of a list of indicators to ensure projects were on course.

With Chris as evaluation coach, I met early on with police command staff and with union leaders to identify desirable outcomes, along with indicators, that were most meaningful to them. This process identified the two highest priorities as raising internal morale and strengthening community relations. For Thin Blue Lines to have credibility and value, these outcomes would need to be at the center of the work and the focus of evaluation. But it was only after they had gone through that process—followed by my outlining how an art project might drive those outcomes—that they realized, "This just might work."

Working with artists working in municipal culture—selection, training, assisting, and appreciating

Three criteria helped me select the poets: excellence in their craft, a level of self-confidence that permitted them to focus on their partner (and not expect attention), and a willingness and ability to follow policies, procedures, and someone else's direction. This last criterion was extremely important in light of the potential consequences in two very different cultures. People working in public service positions are working in hyper-vulnerable settings. Actions, opinions, decisions are constantly scrutinized by the media and the community. It is a culture with a myriad of things to remain mindful of—public perceptions, political considerations, unintended consequences, and a host of complex interpersonal dynamics.

A story and two examples: Before the poets ever met the police officers, they each agreed, upon my asking, that they would not quote their own poetry to their police partner. At our first meeting with the command staff, one of the poets broke his word and enthusiastically quoted a short poem. In seconds, the emotional tenor of the officers went from guarded interest to ice cold "save yourself" shutdown. It was quite dramatic. All the other poets took note. 1) A photographer is on a ride-along that suddenly becomes dangerous. Will he obey as commanded and stay in the cruiser? 2) A story exchange with supervisors and rank-and-file reveals a troubling labor issue. What is good policy when poems include information that might impact personnel career decisions?

Project goals and art: keep the bar high

Questions about quality in community arts projects are valuable and appropriate. After working decades in both professional theater and community arts, I have learned that insisting on excellence is essential to achieving valuable outcomes. I also know that "excellence" is a mutable concept that depends tremendously on context. Keeping the "art bar" high for the officers as well as their partner poets is a sign of respect, the kind of respect and expectation that turns historically low morale into durable pride. The same is true of project goals.

Much to my delight, the police chief agreed to write a poem for our second calendar. Scheduling kept him from attending the workshops held for officers and poets. He ended up writing his poem the night before our deadline. The next morning he confidently announced to his lieutenant that he was "done." The lieutenant told me later that afternoon that he had laughed and said to the chief, "You have no idea." Five rewrites later, the chief's poem was accepted in the calendar.

CREATIVE PLACEMAKING WITH PEOPLE AT THE CENTER

As this project demonstrates, creative placemaking with people at the center recognizes that the most valuable asset any city has is its human capital. It recognizes that creativity is not only one of humanity's most powerful, versatile gifts, it is a part of who we are. Art At Work projects in Portland, Maine, and Holyoke, Massachusetts, have helped change the way people behave, interact, and perceive possibilities. People touched by any of our Thin Blue Lines projects have higher expectations of the police now. They not only have a far more accurate understanding and appreciation of police work, they assume the possibility of a personal relationship that goes beyond enforcement and protection. It is a difference that affects the officers as well. They have shared their lives publicly, their experiences growing up, their struggles as parents, their fears as police officers. They have shown themselves to the community—including our immigrant and refugee youth—in ways other police departments never have. And that makes a decisive difference to everyone.

Our brilliance, resilience, cooperative natures, and willingness to work hard as residents of neighborhoods and cities are all enhanced by figuring out new ways to integrate creative engagement into building a more equitable and sustainable future. This is the kind of work that depends on our ability to step outside our comfort zones, work together, think outside the box, and keep the bar high. What Art At Work and other projects around the country have helped make happen is only a modest start to what is possible.

This is the kind of work that depends on our ability to step outside our comfort zones, work together, think outside the box, and keep the bar high.

Marty Pottenger has been a theater artist, animateur, and social practitioner since 1975, and is the founding director of Art At Work (AAW), a national initiative that increases cities' resilience through strategic art projects addressing social challenges. AAW partners with municipal/county governments, unions, community organizations, and artists.

Cultural Roots, Regrowth, and Resilience

BY MAYOR MITCHELL LANDRIEU

TEN YEARS AGO, NEW ORLEANS experienced one of the most costly manmade disasters in United States history. In total, Hurricane Katrina and its aftermath claimed more than 1,800 American lives and led to $150 billion in damages. In the immediate aftermath, the city's cultural landscape was severely damaged, and left without the artists, musicians, Mardi Gras Indians, and other cultural practitioners that brought the city to life. There were many who thought that New Orleans would never recover.

But in the years immediately following 2005, even as many struggled to return, the community demanded cultural preservation and restoration. Cultural practitioners and producers began to work together to develop plans to restore and simultaneously reinvent the cultural infrastructure of the city. Without this underlying community force, any policy or program would not have succeeded.

When I entered the mayor's office in 2010, the community—not just the cultural community but diverse interest groups from across the entire city—had many competing plans outlining the best way to bring New Orleans back. However, there was little to no buy-in from city government for any of them nor any strategy for implementation. As a first step, I realized we needed to organize and funnel that creative energy onto platforms that would culminate in policy results, and formed transition teams focused on core issues that the city was facing, including neighborhood development and cultural economy. These teams in particular focused on place-based development and a holistic view of culture, cultural businesses, and economic development. Each team created comprehensive and concrete policy plans that were informed by public comments and ready for implementation when I took office. Once in office, I created two new entities to

support the execution of those plans—the Office of Cultural Economy and the Office of Facilities, Infrastructure, and Community Development—with a focus on place-based planning.

CULTURAL ECONOMY OFFICE

The Cultural Economy Office utilizes a two-pronged approach to supporting and nurturing cultural activity and industry in the city through policy and outreach. Policy approaches include streamlining processes that are relevant to cultural activities like special event permitting; creating guides and holding seminars for cultural businesses on licensing and navigating city processes like zoning approvals; the creation of licenses for the purposes of creating legal paths to continuing current cultural business activity; and compiling and publishing data on the cultural economy, such as annual sales revenue, number of businesses, nonprofit activity, and much more. This data provides nonprofits and businesses with important information for decisions, including programming focus or outlet location, on public and private grants.

Victor Harris, Spirit of Fi Yi Yi, Chief of the Mandingo Warriors Mardi Gras Indian tribe, coming out the front door of a home in New Orleans' 7th Ward neighborhood where he grew up, and meeting an ecstatic waiting crowd celebrating Carnival Day on Tuesday, February 28, 2006, about six months after the post-Katrina levee breaks when 80 percent of the city flooded.
PHOTO BY JEFFREY DAVID EHRENREICH

Outreach offers both logistical and financial support for cultural activities and businesses. Since 2010, we have worked successfully with Mardi Gras Indians and Social Aid and Pleasure Clubs to integrate their parade and gathering plans with relevant city agencies, especially the New Orleans Police Department. Indians and Clubs are indigenous New Orleans cultural traditions that serve our neighborhoods not only through annual parades and cultural events, but also by providing social services and support to their members and communities. It is important for the government to provide a supportive infrastructure for these groups, establishing a positive relationship, so that they function through coordination rather than enforcement. One way we do this is through regular participation in Indians and Clubs annual meetings and roundtable discussions.

It is essential for the government to work with communities to help them have the cultural events that create meaning and unity for their residents.

Outreach also includes a small grant program that supports many nonprofit programs throughout the city, particularly those that train workers in cultural industries like film, music, and art teaching, as well as programs that support youth art education. By providing this support, my administration is connected to the cultural community and also crafts programs targeting particular sectors of the cultural economy, such as the film industry.

FACILITIES, INFRASTRUCTURE, AND COMMUNITY DEVELOPMENT OFFICE

The Office of Facilities, Infrastructure, and Community Development has a director of place-based planning who ensures a neighborhood-focused approach to capital projects, oversees grant applications that integrate place-based elements, and coordinates with other offices, including Cultural Economy, when projects require both place-based and cultural elements. One example of this coordination is the creation of the Cultural Economy Planning Map, an interactive web tool that integrates traditional planning data like zoning, schools, and infrastructure with cultural business, nonprofit, and activity data; this tool allows all city departments to integrate culture and place into planning projects.

CONCLUSION

To create a nurturing environment for culture, a city needs to provide both the policy infrastructure to allow for the continued growth of indigenous cultural activity and the outreach programs to integrate cultural interests into programming and decision-making. Tracking cultural activity and economy can also help assimilate culture into the everyday workings of government and give a voice to the community, keeping its interest strong in preserving and fostering local culture.

In New Orleans, we have a rich soil of indigenous culture to work with and an enthusiastic, vocal community with deeply rooted interests in culture. But without policies or outreach efforts that support cultural activity, the seeds of that culture could not continue to grow. New Orleans culture has come back since 2005 because it never fully disappeared. It has grown stronger and bigger than before because we have learned how to support and nourish it, rather than to control it.

It is essential to provide cultural producers, workers, and business owners with the tools that they need to be successful when working with government. It is essential for the government to work with communities to help them have the cultural events that create meaning and unity for their residents. If you do this, you too can watch culture flourish in your city.

Mitchell Landrieu is the mayor of New Orleans, and under his leadership New Orleans has become one of the fastest-growing major cities in America. Prior to being mayor, Landrieu served as Louisiana's lieutenant governor and launched the Cultural Economy Initiative. Mayor Landrieu has a background in theater and was a practicing attorney for 15 years.

Connecting Neighborhoods through Public Art

GREENSBORO, NC

During the dedication of _Over.Under.Pass_ in Greensboro, North Carolina.
PHOTO BY
LYNN DONOVAN
PHOTOGRAPHY

THE CITY OF GREENSBORO HAS A POPULATION of more than 277,000 that is more racially diverse (56 percent white and 33 percent African-American) and slightly younger (a median age of 36) than many other cities in North Carolina. Greensboro's city center is its central business district and serves as both an engine of employment and an important cultural destination, with several historic sites, cultural destinations, and museums in the area. However, for decades, an overpass of a North Carolina Railroad line running parallel to a large four-lane road has acted as a barrier between the city center and the historically underserved, predominantly African-American neighborhoods to the south. This lack of connection is problematic not only because of the disjuncture it causes but also because it has reinforced historic social and racial divisions.

In general, Greensboro is a car city with poorly developed pedestrian networks. To remedy this, following the city's Center City Master Plan, Action Greensboro—a local nonprofit focused on economic, educational, and cultural development in the city—established the Downtown Greenway Project in collaboration with the City of Greensboro. The Downtown Greenway is a planned four-mile walking and biking trail. It will loop around the city center and use public art to engage residents in a unique and authentic way. The intent of the project is to transform the urban landscape, re-establish connections within the diverse community, and promote health and wellness through physical activity.

↑
Evening view of
Over.Under.Pass.
PHOTO BY PETER VAHAN

Public art, selected by the Downtown Greenway Art Selection Panel, which consists of community stakeholders, elected officials, and city staff, has been and will be installed at key sites determined by the project team. The hope is that each piece will activate and encourage use of the Greenway as an alternative means of transportation. One of the art commissions, *Over.Under.Pass*, was installed in the previously mentioned abandoned underpass—near the Morehead Park section of the greenway. Its name is meant to signal the transformation of the railway overpass from a barrier to a point of connectivity.

Community dialogue was an important aspect of the project. To ensure community participation in the planning process, Greensboro Neighborhood Congress helped the project team to organize citizens and public meetings. Public meetings were held in schools, churches, and community centers, places easy for community members to access. The information gleaned at these meetings was used to inform the design of the greenway and its public art commissions.

As a true public/private partnership project, partners also have worked closely with numerous city government agencies, including the Parks & Recreation and Planning, Police, and Transportation Departments, to gather support from local foundations and corporate supporters as well as private investors. With $6.5 million invested to date on the project, Greensboro has secured over $200 million in completed and planned investment.

The economic impact of the greenway has already exceeded expectations and spurred other area community development. Greensboro's Parks & Recreation Department tracks trail use. Analysis of the data indicates higher pathway use of the Morehead Park section compared to others in the citywide system. Numbers and time-of-day usage also indicate that the *Over.Under.Pass* pathway is being used by downtown visitors and commuters as an alternate route into and out of the city and not just for recreational purposes, although an unanticipated level of enthusiasm has sprung up around using the greenway for organized fitness events. Overall, the Downtown Greenway project has activated the area, helping to enhance relationships between area neighborhoods and businesses.

The greenway trail system is just over 18 percent complete with three-quarters of a mile of finished trails. To ensure that current and future public art installations are well-kept, an endowment has been created by project managers to fund the maintenance of all public art; maintenance funding is a common challenge for public art projects. As it is an integral aspect of the project, the Downtown Greenway Project continues to reinforce the value of public art and the continued opportunity it presents to redefine and revitalize Greensboro.

Community Building via Public Art in Public Housing

BY DAVID HANEY

HOUSING IS A KEY COMPONENT OF COMMUNITY development. Critical to the development of strong communities is housing that is safe, decent, and affordable. However, there are many other elements that make a "house" a "home."

HOUSING THE ART OF POSSIBILITY

In early 2011, Wyoming Community Development Authority (WCDA) identified a unique opportunity to integrate public art into a new development for low-income affordable housing when the property they were developing with Grimshaw Investments in Casper, Wyoming, was located directly across the street from the Nicolaysen Art Museum (NIC). WCDA and NIC, in collaboration with Grimshaw and the City of Casper, developed the Housing the Art of Possibility public art concept. As part of the project, they envisioned the placement of public art next to the new affordable housing project, Sunshine Apartments. Centered on sustainability in its broadest sense, the project used recycled materials from the demolition of a condemned multifamily property, replaced the original dilapidated residences with LEED-certified affordable housing, and developed the property around which the public art piece would sit. This work was made possible by federal Neighborhood Stabilization Funding provided to Grimshaw by WCDA.

The group also applied for and was awarded two grants, one from the National Endowment for the Arts Our Town grant program and the other from the Wyoming Arts Council, to develop the public art piece and its accompanying programming; both applications were written by NIC. Selected by the group as a whole through a request for proposal process led by NIC, artist Mathew Dehaemers designed, fabricated, and installed his artwork, a vast sundial

Confluence of Time and Space, **an interactive public sculpture by Matthew Dahaemers in Casper, Wyoming.**
PHOTO COURTESY OF NICOLAYSEN ART MUSEUM AND THE ARTIST

titled *Confluence of Time and Place*, in the new public space. The piece incorporates Wyoming's rich history of natural resources and geological topography, using recycled glass to fill the sides that are illuminated by colored lights at night. Now that the project is complete, the City of Casper has been deeded the land for the park and agreed to maintain it in perpetuity.

WHAT DID WE LEARN?

1. Every project needs a champion. Leadership by WCDA was key to the success of the project.

2. It takes a very broad coalition of players to create a valuable community asset. Our partners included an established developer, the city government, federal partners, local philanthropic entities, and the local arts community.

3. All partners must be willing to think out-of-the-box, to stretch themselves well beyond their traditional roles and comfort zones. Those not in the art business have to learn how artists

work and create. Those in the art business have to learn how to work within a larger development project and collaborate on a business and financial plateau not in their normal day-to-day operations. There is a learning curve for both arts and non-arts partners.

4. It is important to engage collaborators with a high level of expertise within their particular specialty; not just anyone will do. Collaborators were chosen from the developer, city government, federal partners, local philanthropic entities, and the local art community.

5. The project team must engage the community in project activities, including working to better ensure that residents are invested in the outcome. As part of this, the arts community must educate the non-arts community on their process and how best to interact with artists.

Working with the local arts community can lead to long-term relationships between artists and community, helping to situate the arts more firmly into the community fabric.

6. All opinions must be respected to assure that the outcome represents the broadest range of stakeholders possible.

7. At least one partner, preferably from the local arts community, needs to be well-versed in the process of artist/artwork solicitation and selection. This expertise includes both conceptualization and execution within a prescribed budget.

WHAT ARE THE BENEFITS OF A HOUSING AUTHORITY DOING PUBLIC ART?

1. Public art is both ornamental and practical. It can lead not only to improved area aesthetics but also to increased area foot traffic and reduced crime, improving quality of life for residents.

2. The design and process of creating public art can capitalize on historic, economic, and community circumstances to enhance community cohesion.

3. Working with the local arts community can lead to long-term relationships between artists and the community, helping to situate the arts more firmly into the community fabric. For example, this project prompted the creation of several educational arts outreach programs that engage community members of all ages in hands-on creative arts activities related to public art, sustainability, and the environment.

4. Public art can act as an economic driver to strengthen weak local markets. For instance, the east end of the redevelopment area of downtown lacked a quality anchor to stabilize a deteriorating and blighted neighborhood, but due to the Housing the Art of Possibility project it has made the area one of the preferred locations in the city of Casper.

In tandem with area redevelopment, the Housing the Art of Possibility project has enhanced the visual landscape and character of the area surrounding the Sunshine Apartments housing complex. It has created a gathering place for the community, especially residents of Sunshine Apartments and Skyline Towers, the adjacent senior housing project. Through Housing the Art of Possibility, the group has been able to provide the Casper community with a source of community pride. The ultimate vision for this area is to create a sustainable community area by uniting education, art, housing, transportation, and walkability while encouraging the preservation and beautification of the downtown area through development, reuse, and redevelopment, and it has succeeded.

The breadth of the local partnerships supported not only a piece of public art but also the integration of art with housing, the inclusion of new green space, youth art education, and a variety of multi-generational gathering opportunities. *Confluence of Time and Place* successfully brought together a community and its built environment in an outstanding display of community development incorporating the arts.

David Haney is the former executive director of the Wyoming Community Development Authority. A nationally recognized leader in community and economic development, Haney brought extensive expertise to the WCDA through his work and community service in both workforce housing and the banking industry.

How Can Working with the Federal Government Advance Creative Placemaking Locally?

BY JENNIFER HUGHES

OVER THE LAST SIX YEARS, CREATIVE PLACEMAKING is a term that has caught fire and sparked the interest of a range of sectors, everything from public safety to public health. The widespread adoption of creative placemaking as a local strategy for building community and igniting the local economy was in response to federal and foundation funding opportunities, and driven by local innovators that rejected one-size-fits-all solutions of the past that were not responsive to the specific needs of their place.

A BIT OF HISTORY

Federal government policies of the past have shaped the built environment in ways that have exacerbated inequality. Broad sweeping policies, such as building highways that divided cities and cookie-cutter housing policies that resulted in public housing superblocks, neglected to acknowledge and account for the people and uniqueness of each place. The good news is that over the last several years, the federal government has been rethinking its role and redesigning its programs to be more responsive to the specific needs of places. In addition, a subset of the federal workforce has been trained to pivot from in-the-box, program-driven roles to be more holistic funders and supporters of place-based innovations and ideas. Recognizing that local communities and residents have the answers and tools to help restitch, rebuild, and reconnect their communities, the federal government has been delivering programs that respect and privilege local knowledge.

In addition, other sectors are beginning to recognize the potential for arts-driven community work to move the needle in their mission areas. White House place-based initiatives, like Promise Zones and Strong Cities Strong Communities, have helped to illuminate how federal agencies working together can have greater impact,

> Recognizing that local communities and residents have the answers and tools to help restitch, rebuild, and reconnect their communities, the federal government has been delivering programs that respect and privilege local knowledge.

Bhutanese youth
participate in
"We Are Portland,"
a project capturing
the faces and stories
of a changing
Portland, Oregon.
PHOTO COURTESY OF
MY STORY

and how arts and culture play a central role in the success of local community development so that a zip code does not determine a child's destiny.

ENGAGING THE FEDERAL GOVERNMENT LOCALLY

As you embark on a local creative placemaking project, how do you leverage federal government resources, to build capacity and support locally for arts interventions? An even more burning question might be: What can the federal government do to help advance your local creative placemaking work?

Here are some ways to get started:

1. Recognize that the federal government has more to offer than dollars. Financial resources are certainly necessary to carry out community projects, but money is not the only ingredient for a successful creative placemaking intervention. The federal government can also provide technical assistance and information on background research, case studies, and toolkits for success.

2. Get to know your local, regional, state, and federal staff. Building relationships is an important investment of time and energy. Not every investment of your time will pay off; however, the more you can establish relationships with federal staff within your region and at headquarters, the more likely you will discover how your arts and cultural intervention intersects with their mission. Public servants can be cheerleaders for the work you are doing on the ground and be the conduit for new connections and national networks of learning. As a national funder, the federal government can be an informative source for best practices and inspiring ideas, and can connect you with local work happening in all corners of the country. You may discover new ways of financing your project work along the way, too.

3. Share your story, local narrative, and challenges on an ongoing basis. As a federal grant program manager, I spend a good deal of my time presenting and talking about the work that we fund to varied audiences. The federal government can help to amplify the work that you are doing to a national audience. Your challenges and successes can also help to inform the ways that projects and programs are funded moving forward. As you learn about what works and doesn't on the ground, share that information with federal colleagues. You have an opportunity to help drive federal government research agendas and grant guidelines that might better advance policy and enable the important work you are doing to drive community outcomes. Lifting up stories about what is working and what isn't helps others learn from your experience, so share freely and often.

The onus is also on us as a federal workforce to engage more directly with the local work impacted by federal dollars and policy, and to proactively seek out ways that we can better serve the American public.

4. Position your creative placemaking work in a way that helps advance the mission of various federal and government agencies. Each government agency has a specific mission and range of tools to support local community work. For example, while the U.S. Department of Agriculture Rural Development program does offer competitive grant opportunities, the majority of its financial support is delivered through loans and providing access to capital in communities that would not otherwise be able to access it. Understanding the levers and realms of influence of various federal agencies will enable you to better position your project for future support. Depending on

the target audience, you might choose to focus on how artists in your community are impacting local food systems or how a performance project might bring new residents to the table of a planning process.

While these are some quick suggestions for those working locally, the onus is also on us as a federal workforce to engage more directly with the local work impacted by federal dollars and policy, and to proactively seek out ways that we can better serve the American public. In partnership, we can help move the needle on how creative placemaking is understood, impacts local communities, and enhances the lives of all Americans.

Jennifer Hughes is the community solutions specialist at the National Endowment for the Arts, overseeing the NEA's creative placemaking grant program, Our Town, as well as the Mayors' Institute on City Design and Citizens' Institute on Rural Design. Hughes serves as a resource member on the White House Council for Strong Cities Strong Communities and Promise Zones teams, advising U.S. communities on arts, cultural, and design strategies that drive economic and neighborhood revitalization.

Chapter 5

arts + physical infrastructure

Cultural Building Projects: Guidelines for Planning

BY JOANNA WORONKOWICZ

AS A CITY OR CULTURAL LEADER, you've probably heard that many places across the U.S. are building cultural facilities as means to promote tourism, enrich citizen cultural life, or provide amenities for workers being recruited by area businesses. Perhaps you, or your city, have even considered building a new or renovating an existing cultural facility for one of these very reasons. If so, you may be seeking advice on how to ensure that your cultural building project is a successful one.

Embarking on a cultural building project is a huge endeavor—one that should not be taken lightly. On average, a cultural building project takes around nine years (and sometimes as many as 15 years) from the time the planning group decides on a budget to opening the doors of a new or renovated facility. It was no joke when one director of a recently completed cultural building project commented, "It takes nerves of steel," referring to the process that he went through.

That being said, if after considering the time, energy, and (of course) money it takes to build a cultural facility, you've decided that it's something your city will benefit from, please consider the following planning dos and don'ts that can help ensure a smooth process.

DO GATHER DATA

Understanding the experiences of others who have built cultural facilities is key to planning your own project. In other words, don't try to reinvent the wheel. Your job, as a project leader, is to survey the field and talk to as many people as possible who have built similar facilities. Ask about every detail of the planning process, from how long construction took to the amount the budget increased by (because it will happen) to how much the facility cost

Rendering of community gathering in Writers Theatre lobby in Glencoe, Illinois.
IMAGE COURTESY OF STUDIO GANG ARCHITECTS

to manage after it was complete. Get as many opinions as possible and try not to rely on one more than another (especially if it's your own). If you hire a consultant, make sure to compare his opinion to others. By gathering data, you can try to anticipate the way things can go wrong and, more importantly, plan for it.

DO HAVE A BUSINESS PLAN

It sounds simple, but having a business plan before starting a cultural building project is an incredibly effective way to make sure things go smoothly. A business plan not only outlines the steps of the project but also puts in writing why the project is being pursued. Considering how long it takes to complete a cultural building project, it's very easy for those involved to forget the initial motivations behind one. For example, a performing arts center may have originally been planned to provide performance space for local area arts groups. Yet, after the challenges of paying for maintenance of the facility became more apparent, the performing arts center now primarily rents space to out-of-town touring acts and conventions.

A business plan can also help with setting measurable goals. Perhaps the planning group made a decision to not break ground until all of the money for construction was raised, but certain members of the group are getting impatient with how long the fundraising process is taking. Including these types of goals, and others, can help prevent project planners from taking steps they're not ready for. Finally, a business plan can be a mechanism for broadcasting the responsibilities of the leadership group and holding leaders accountable. More importantly, a plan can help facilitate collaboration—by understanding what tasks remain, planning group members can offer their skills and expertise where needed.

DON'T IGNORE THE OPPOSITION

It's often easier not to listen when someone tells you that you're wrong, or how you're doing something may be hindering other people's interests, for listening generally requires changing your course of action, making things less convenient as a result. Nevertheless, the opposition may have good advice to offer that in the end can help ensure the outcome of a project. When planning for a cultural building project, it's important to offer safe forums in which people can dissent, such as a public meeting or informal interview with community residents. Not only can project leaders learn something they didn't know about how to build a successful project, but giving the opposition the opportunity to be heard can help prevent more opposition, and a more difficult process, down the line.

> Get as many opinions as possible and try not to rely on one more than another (especially if it's your own).

DON'T BUILD FOR THE WRONG REASONS

We've all now heard the famous mantra "If you build it, they will come" applied to cultural building projects. For cultural leaders, this mantra elicits visions of swarming crowds at a new cultural facility. For city leaders, there are visions of bustling city sidewalks, new restaurants and businesses, all adding to a city's economic development. As attractive as all of this may sound, unfortunately, there's very little evidence that building a cultural facility will result in a heightened level of economic activity for the long-term. More likely what will happen is a short-term increase in audiences who come to experience the new building. It's possible that more cultural amenities may spur investment in other types of complementary business as well. However, in order for this to happen, a cultural building project should be a smaller part of a larger economic development plan with many pieces that must fall into place beforehand.

In conclusion, cultural building projects can help strengthen communities and organizations, but only if their leaders pursue projects responsibly. Otherwise, building projects have the potential to wreak havoc on organizational or municipal finances, and community morale. Using the resources available to help guide cultural building projects can seriously improve the chances of a project being successful.

Resources on Cultural Facility Building

Frumkin, P. and A. Kolendo. *Building for the Arts: The Strategic Design of Cultural Facilities*. University of Chicago Press. 2014.

Woronkowicz, J., D.C. Joynes, and N. Bradburn. *Building Better Arts Facilities: Lessons from a U.S. National Study*. Routledge. 2014.

Woronkowicz, J., et al. *Set in Stone: Building America's New Generation of Cultural Facilities*. University of Chicago. 2012. Available at http://culturalpolicy.uchicago.edu/setinstone/pdf/setinstone.pdf

Joanna Woronkowicz is an assistant professor in the School of Public and Environmental Affairs at Indiana University in Bloomington, where she conducts research in cultural policy and nonprofit management. Before Indiana University, Woronkowicz served as the senior research officer at the National Endowment for the Arts.

Designing and Activating Public Space

JACKSON, MS

SITUATED ON THE BANKS OF THE PEARL RIVER, Jackson is Mississippi's state capital and a major transportation and commerce hub. It is the state's largest city, with a population of more than a half-million residents in the larger metropolitan region. Jackson and the state of Mississippi continue to confront challenges from their segregated history. However, in spite of, and often because of, this turbulent past, many Mississippians have created profound literature and music. Following these traditions, Jackson is home to a growing community of cultural and educational organizations.

Today, downtown Jackson is experiencing a renaissance and becoming more of a mixed-use community. In the last several years, a cluster of cultural organizations has formed near the Jackson Convention Complex in downtown Jackson to create the Midtown Arts District. Institutions include the Mississippi Museum of Art (MMA), the Thalia Mara Hall, and the Mississippi Arts Center. Even with all this redevelopment, however, the area lacked outdoor public gathering spaces.

Shortly after moving to its current downtown location in 2007, MMA sought to remedy this by transforming a retired 1.2-acre city-owned parking lot that sat adjacent to its building into an open public park with a lawn and a performance space. The park gives Jackson residents, workers, and visitors a central social space to enjoy their lunch breaks, meet up with friends, or relax after hours. It also provides a venue for the museum and other area arts groups to hold public performances and programs to more directly engage the community with art and entice new audience members.

The park opened in September 2011 after three years of planning and almost a year of construction. Partners in this effort included

**Visitors and artists
in the Art Garden
outside of the
Mississippi Museum
of Art.**
PHOTO BY
JULIAN RANKIN

MMA, City of Jackson, and Downtown Jackson Partners, a local
nonprofit that works to attract and retain businesses in the area.
As the first green space to open in the downtown area since the
1970s, the park, or Art Garden, serves as an invaluable civic space
for those living downtown and throughout Jackson, as well as
visitors and theater goers. It also ties together the various artistic
and cultural buildings and organizations that reside downtown.

The Art Garden houses intimate outdoor galleries, "classrooms,"
performance spaces, outdoor terrace dining, native garden beds,
and soothing fountains. Programming for the venue is provided
by area cultural organizations, including Mississippi Symphony
Orchestra, Mississippi Opera, Ballet Mississippi, Crossroads
Film Society, and the Greater Jackson Arts Council. It includes
performances, rehearsals, music and dance lessons, festivals,
movie screenings, and farmers markets. To ensure the Art Garden's
maintenance in perpetuity, MMA has established an endowment to
fund its upkeep and future improvements.

Children playing in the Art Garden.
PHOTO BY
JULIAN RANKIN

Altogether, having diverse partnerships and developing diverse programs for a range of audiences has helped to broaden the appeal of both the park and downtown Jackson and enhanced the livability of the district. According to audience surveys: 67 percent of the people attending evening and weekend events do not live or work in downtown Jackson, many living outside of the city itself; 99 percent of respondents said they were "extremely satisfied" with the park; and 19 percent of visitors indicated that the performance they had attended was their first downtown cultural event. Though MMA did advertise, the survey also showed that many participants had discovered the park and its related programming through social means; over 50 percent of respondents indicated they had found out by word-of-mouth. From this, it is evident that the park has achieved the project goal of creating central social space for residents and visitors to relax and enjoy the outdoors in downtown Jackson.

Five Lessons Learned for a Successful Public Art Project

BY PATRICIA WALSH

Community engagement is a key component to a successful public art project.

PUBLIC ART CAN PLAY A UNIQUE ROLE in a place by providing a platform to explore community identity, engage the local arts and cultural sector, offer a space for civic dialogue, and enhance appreciation for art—to name just a few of its benefits. The process and outcomes for each public art project and program vary from city to city, town to town, community to community—however there are some fundamental lessons that have been learned over the years by public art professionals working in the field. Here are some lessons I have found to be true no matter the size of the budget, the final outcome of the project, or the community where the artwork lives.

1. **The Public Comes First in Public Art:** Community engagement is a key component to a successful public art project. The engagement process can vary from a broad public meeting to a community-based committee or public contribution to the creation of the artwork. Whatever is the case for your project, it is important to ensure that the community is providing input into the final outcome. Their engagement in development of a public artwork can equate to the long-term success of the project. Part of this success requires having an artist who is open to working with the community when developing a project. How the artist works with the community can vary from direct engagement to conceptual input in the design.

    The need for community input was evident during my time as collection manager with the San Jose public art program. As this position required field work, it was clearly visible when an artwork was loved by the community. I remember cleaning graffiti from a beloved mosaic dog sculpture, and the outrage that the community felt from the damage done to the work.

Arts engagement with seniors as a part of "New Hampshire Ave: This Is a Place To..." in Takoma Park, Maryland.
PHOTO BY BEN CARVER

Typically, while working in the field few members of the public approached me, but during the time I spent cleaning that sculpture I had several community members come to me and express how upset they were about the damage. They told me about their experience working with the artist and how they contributed pieces of porcelain and tile from their own homes for the mosaic. This type of dedication depicts the role that public art can play in the development of civic pride and care for one's environment, and how the community's engagement can help ensure the care of the artwork.

2. **The Process is Equally as Important as the Outcome:**
    We all love to see the end of a project, and having an object that emulates the community can be a testament to the work accomplished during the process. How a public artwork is developed and implemented can have much bearing on the long-term success of a project. Take the example listed above. How would the reaction of the community have changed if they did not have an attachment to the work? What if the artist

and artwork were selected from a catalogue and place in the community without notice or engagement? Would there have been outrage toward the graffiti or perhaps instead a call for the removal of the artwork? Without a process to engage the community, to select an artist who can work with the public and is open to input from the public, the project, though well-intentioned, may never be embraced by the community.

3. **Plan for the Care and Maintenance of a Public Artwork:** Over the years it has become more and more apparent that public artworks, like all public assets and facilities, need a plan and funding for long-term care. Planning for the care of the artwork can include annual maintenance, regular conservation efforts, and plans for repairs and other damage that can occur throughout the life cycle of the artwork. As mentioned above, even if an artwork is well cared for by the community, it can still be victim to damage. Hence, another consideration when looking at the care of an artwork is the expected lifespan. For the artwork mentioned above there was already a plan in place and precautions taken prior to the inflicted damage. Some of the precautions included covering the artwork in a sealant that worked as a graffiti abatement coating, consulting with conservators to develop a plan for the care of the artwork, and securing an emergency fund for artworks that may need triage work outside of their regularly scheduled maintenance.

> This lesson is one of the most important I have learned over my ten-year career—hire a public art professional when embarking on a public art project.

4. **Hire a Professional:** Community engagement, artist's management, fabrication, site installation, maintenance—much goes into the planning and implementation of a public artwork. There have been years of growth and understanding of best practices in the field of public art. This lesson is one of the most important I have learned over my ten-year career—hire a public art professional when embarking on a public art project. From understanding the funding to artist's management and the legal aspects of commissioning an artwork, there are professional consultants who can help you with your project.

An additional note on working with artists: Seasoned public art professionals can work with artists with varied degrees of field experience. This experience can be beneficial in a number of ways including training local artists to work in the public art field and attracting successful artists to complete new works.

5. **Controversies are Opportunities:** It is true that public art can be a lightning rod for discourse and controversy, however these issues are not reasons to shy away from a community engagement process or avoid public art altogether. It is an opportunity to further connect with the community and understand their issues. Each public art project is unique because of the collective efforts put forth to make the projects happen. Controversies can occur on multiple levels from community reactions and interdepartmental communication challenges to political movement from elected bodies. These challenges can kick up some dust, but know that you are not alone and this is part of the process.

For more than 15 years, the public art field has had a national ally from Americans for the Arts in the form of the Public Art Network (PAN). PAN is the only national network of public art professionals in the United States dedicated to advancing public art programs and projects through advocacy, policy, and information resources to further art and design in our built environment. Public art professionals have been working in and building the field for decades. PAN develops professional services for the broad array of individuals and organizations engaged in the diverse field of public art. To learn more about PAN please visit www. AmericansfortheArts.org/PAN and feel free to reach out to us at pan@artsusa.org.

Patricia Walsh is the public art programs manager at Americans for the Arts. Her background includes the conservation and maintenance of a public artwork collection, working on community engagement initiatives, and managing temporary public art projects.

Restoring Folk Art Is Creating Jobs and Revitalizing a Downtown

WILSON, NC

ONCE HOME TO A THRIVING TOBACCO INDUSTRY, Wilson is a small city of just under 50,000 people in rural North Carolina. The most recent census shows a diverse population of about 42 percent Caucasian, 47 percent African-American, and 10 percent Hispanic or Latino residents. Following the federal tobacco buy-out program, many of Wilson's international tobacco buyers who were central to the region's economy stopped coming to the city, leaving an economic vacuum. Today, 19.5 percent of Wilson residents live below poverty level, and the median household income is $38,384.

Recently, Wilson was gifted ownership of a collection of large kinetic sculptures inspired by windmills. Created by the late WWII veteran Vollis Simpson, these "whirligigs" are internationally celebrated examples of vernacular art, and part of museum collections across the country, including the American Visionary Art Museum in Baltimore. The donated sculptures are in need of serious conservation as they are housed outdoors and have many moving parts which have deteriorated over the years. (As Simpson's health declined, he was subsequently unable to manage their upkeep; Simpson passed away at the age of 94 in 2013.)

Working in public-private partnership, Wilson Downtown Properties (a nonprofit organization that encourages community development in Wilson's downtown), the North Carolina Arts Council, and the City of Wilson set out to conserve the whirligigs and exhibit them in a new central public park. To anchor and activate underutilized civic space, the park would be located in the heart of Historic Downtown Wilson, close to the train station and Wilson's administrative offices, and accessible to residents and visitors alike. (Each year the annual Whirligig Festival draws about 50,000 people to town.)

From the beginning, job training in conservation, engineering, and mechanics was identified as an area of importance to the project.

To develop its workforce-training program, the team collaborated with St. John's Community Development Corporation, Opportunities Industrialization Center of Wilson, and the Wilson Community College, and targeted the local under/unemployed college-age youth population. With a mind toward preservation and mechanical craftsmanship, individuals took classes in welding, metal fabrication, sanding, grinding, painting, documentation, photography, and/or record-keeping. Conservation experts were hired by the project partners to guide the process and help establish high standards and protocols for mechanical and surface treatments; the intent was for these protocols to serve as a national model for conservation of vernacular art. Youth enrolled in the training were then hired and trained by the project to work on the whirligigs with the conservation experts. To date, the project has created 25 jobs as part of its workforce-training program, and has finished conserving 23 of the whirligigs.

The conservation facility for Vollis Simpson's artworks.
PHOTO COURTESY OF VOLLIS SIMPSON WHIRLGIG PARK PROJECT

The completed restoration of these iconic structures marks the advent of the project phase focused on the development of the public park in downtown Wilson. Project partners initially projected a $40 million dollar increase in private investment in the surrounding area over the ten years following the park's opening. In actuality, before the park's construction has even begun, more than $20 million in private investment has already occurred, including the transformation of long-time vacant properties in Historic Downtown Wilson into mixed-use developments. For example, Nash Street Lofts, a nearly century-old building on Wilson's main thoroughfare, was vacant for more than 20 years but recently was redeveloped. Upon its opening in spring 2014, ten of the 13 units already were rented and occupied. This and other development plans and activities continue to bring new energy to downtown Wilson, adding further cultural resources to the city's holdings and improving its economic future.

A Home for Artists, an Anchor for Community

BY COLIN HAMILTON

Artspace residents at PS109 in East Harlem.
PHOTO BY
JAMES SHANKS

LOWERTOWN WAS A DESOLATE, 18-BLOCK stretch of St. Paul's warehouse district when Artspace opened the Northern Warehouse, a 160,000-square-foot historic building, blending 52 artist live/work units with space for 27 creative enterprises. Over the decades that followed, thanks to the incalculable sweat equity of the many artists who have made it their home, Lowertown has re-emerged as St. Paul's most dynamic neighborhood—with a destination Art Crawl, thriving small businesses, a farmers' market, new residents, and now a minor league ballpark. While this story of artist-led change is hardly unique, it does have a particular silver lining: because of a commitment to permanently affordable artist housing, artists have remained a core part of Lowertown through all its changes.

The Northern Warehouse was the first of almost 40 projects Artspace has developed in communities as varied as New York City and Minot, North Dakota, and the majority of our projects incorporate artist housing. We are pleased to share a small piece of what we have learned.

1. **Stick your toe in first.** Artist housing can anchor a thriving community, but it is also a complicated process and significant investment. Before going too far, do your homework. Some questions to ask include: What are the scale, space needs, and financial limits of your artist community? Are there buildings or lots attractive to the creative community, and can those sites be secured? Is there political leadership to advance a project through its inevitable challenges? Are there financial resources to properly capitalize a development?

2. **Design for the distinct needs of artists.** Successful artist housing is not just housing available to artists; it is housing deliberately designed for artists. We create live/work units with enough additional space (generally 150–200 square feet) to double as working studios. We build around a flexible, open floor plan and lighting systems that allow artists to manipulate space to suit their needs. Durability is key, with materials in flooring, counters, sinks, and others surfaces that can withstand more than the usual wear and tear. We push for ten-foot ceilings complemented by large windows with abundant natural light. Within the building itself, we create complementary spaces that support artistic activity: wide hallways that double as exhibition space, community rooms, and other public spaces that support rehearsals, performances, gatherings, and exhibitions. Oversized doorways and elevators are a must. Brace yourself: artist housing generally costs more than equivalent affordable housing.

> **Successful artist housing is not just housing available to artists; it is housing deliberately designed for artists.**

3. **Run an equitable, community-based selection process.** The majority of our projects are funded in part by Low Income Housing Tax Credits, which are a powerful tool for affordable housing projects but that also impose strict regulations governing the eligibility of applicants. Beyond those, however, a developer can do certain things such as create a "preference" that allows qualifying artists to move to the front of the line. However, an artist preference is just the start. We also do substantial outreach so that artists are aware of the opportunity and know how to navigate the complex, sometimes intimidating application process; in our experience, many artisans and craftspeople do not realize artist housing is for them. To screen applicants, we work with an Artist Selection Committee comprised of local artists. In our review, we are clear that we are not curatorial. Instead we look for individuals with a sustained commitment to their craft; individuals excited about participating in an engaged community; and individuals comfortable living in a building noisier, more lively, and more social than most rental properties.

4. **Embrace a little chaos.** Artist housing requires tolerant management practices. We have many residents who make noise and work odd hours. Our lobbies are the extensions of residents' living rooms, and public hallways are an extension of their identities and creativity. Many residents need to make physical modifications to their spaces. Creative residents can test a property manager's patience. Successful projects are managed by flexibly minded people.

5. **Governance matters.** We ask residents to share in the governance of buildings by participating on committees charged with significant responsibilities, such as planning artistic programming or managing livability issues. In the best projects, residents are invested not just in their own creative exploration, but also with one another and the collective spaces they share.

6. **Commit to the long-term.** As a nonprofit developer, we are committed to permanent affordability for low-income artists. Delivering on this promise requires that most profits generated through rents and leases are reinvested back into the property; that we regularly defer our fees; and that we forgo opportunities to switch to market rates. The margins are very tight. Artspace needs to remain sustainable, but our goal is to create wealth for our host community, not ourselves.

How do you know when you have got it right? How about this from Amontaine Aurore, a resident in our first Seattle project: "When I pass the community room and witness a dancer lengthening and strengthening her muscles or a painter/photographer hanging his eclectic creations in anticipation of First Thursday Art Walk, when I walk down the hallway and from behind closed doors catch the whiff of a singer's trill or a piano's poem, when I stop to chat with my neighbor and she tells me about the triumph of her artist residency and I share the hope/wish/prayer for my latest play, then I often stop, breathe, and think to myself: Ahhh! Home."

Colin Hamilton is senior vice president of national advancement at Artspace, a nonprofit real estate developer that owns and operates more than 40 "art spaces" from coast-to-coast. Prior to joining Artspace, Hamilton led the campaign to fund a new Minneapolis Central Library and capital improvements to each of its branches.

Bringing Historic Structures Back to Life through Artists' Housing

HAMILTON, OH

A SUBURB OF CINCINNATI, OHIO, HAMILTON has a population of 62,000. The Great Miami River, which cuts through the city and its historic downtown, once provided a robust economic engine for shipping and manufacturing. Ornate 19th- and early 20th-century architecture serves as a marker of these industrial boom times. Today, Hamilton is a relatively affordable community with a high quality of life. While Hamilton's population has decreased over the past four decades, its median family income has increased, reaching $49,104 in Hamilton County as of 2012. In 2000, Hamilton implemented a comprehensive planning process, Vision 2020, which created a framework for city planning and policymaking, including a focus on the development and historic preservation of its downtown.

Known as the "City of Sculpture," artists have long helped define Hamilton's downtown area by living and working in what has been a relatively low-rent district, making use of the historic and, in some cases, loft-like spaces. To ensure that artists could remain an integral part of the neighborhood, and help neutralize the risk of gentrification forcing artists out of the neighborhood, the Vision 2020 Commission invited Minneapolis-based Artspace to conduct a feasibility study to determine the needs for affordable artist housing in downtown Hamilton in 2008. The final Arts Market Study indicated strong demand for live/work affordable housing for artists and supported the development of 40-50 live/work units. It also helped to identify more than 5,000 local artists, a roster of local media, and a mailing list of interested community members. Following the study's conclusion, architect Michael Dingeldein of SHP Leading Design was hired to produce conceptual designs to represent possible ways forward. Two community charrettes attended by approximately 60 artists were held to respond to

**Evening view of
artists' housing
façade in
Hamilton, Ohio.**
PHOTO BY
SCOTT MERRILL
PHOTOGRAPHY

the proposed plans and designs and increase the project's and
arts community's visibility. To maximize community engagement,
organizers exhibited the designs in a vacant storefront nearby and
distributed flyers throughout the community and on the Internet
with the assistance of their local partners. Through these efforts,
the project team was able to gain critical insight into community
priorities and culture.

The project team knew that they needed to take extra care
to engage local stakeholders, as local partnerships are key to
ensuring long-term project success. Working with the City of
Hamilton to ensure project plans were consistent with the city's
vision, Artspace established an integrated network of local
stakeholders that included government leaders, members of the
arts community, local developers, and philanthropic organizations.
These partners supported the project in a myriad of ways, including
project management, finance, predevelopment, leasing, monetary
contributions, and avenues of communication to the community.

In April 2013, property was acquired on High Street; built around 1900, the Mehrum and Lindley buildings were internally connected in the 1920s and covered over by panels of metal louvers, completely masking their historic facades, in the 1970s. The project is backed by a variety of financial backing, including Low Income Housing Tax Credits, Community Development Block Grants, HOME Federal Funds, Federal Historic Tax Credits, State of Ohio Historic Tax Credits, and donations from individuals and organizations. Construction was completed in fall 2015, and the building will reach stable operations within five years. Applications for space are accepted on a first come, first served basis. The goal of the project is to provide permanent affordable housing to qualified artists, stabilize a portion of the local arts community, preserve historic structures, bring vacant and/or underutilized spaces back on the tax rolls, foster the safety and livability of neighborhoods (without evidence of gentrification-led displacement), expand public access to the arts, and attract other supporting non-arts businesses to the area.

Artisan Businesses and Equitable Neighborhood Development: An Important Formula

BY ILANA PREUSS

REAL ESTATE PROJECTS AND EQUITABLE neighborhood development benefit from including artisan businesses. These businesses are major assets that draw people to the neighborhood, strengthen the local economy, and can stabilize or increase the value of local real estate. To succeed, this tenant or use-type must be incorporated into community development plans from the start.

WHO ARE THESE BUSINESSES?

Artisan businesses, or maker industries, are stand-alone businesses that produce goods—often by hand or with a small set of tools. They have a few defining characteristics. They are full-time producers, are generally a sole proprietor business or have one or two employees, and sell their goods online or at local markets. These businesses are not major space users. They may be a home-based business that produced jewelry for the past 30 years or a younger business like Stitch & Rivet, a Washington, DC leather goods studio working out of a micro-retail space (less than 500 square feet). They may also be artists-entrepreneurs-community organizers like Tendani Mpulubusi El who has production and event space, with no need for retail frontage.

Most artisan businesses start with about 400 to 600 square feet of space. They may prefer interior or side-street spaces for production-only use, or they may be great micro-retail tenants and produce in their open retail space. Most artisan businesses pay below market-rate prices for their space but are great economic assets to a development project and a neighborhood.

Small business owner displaying her work in Honolulu, Hawaii.
PHOTO COURTESY OF RECAST CITY

WHY ARE THEY IMPORTANT TO LOCAL REAL ESTATE AND ECONOMIC OPPORTUNITY?

Artisan businesses can bring people together, increase economic opportunity in a neighborhood, and help to shine a unique spotlight on the real estate project.

Bringing People Together

Artisan businesses attract people who want to be a part of the creative community and support locally made products. Survey after survey show that people want places to gather and feel included—artisan events are one homegrown way to answer that demand. Both business owners and customers are strengthened through events like local fairs, markets, and festivals that showcase new products from local artisans. Workshops on business development for new and potential artisans also help to bring people together around this topic. These both strengthen the community of producers and promote the local business sector as an employment avenue to more neighbors.

Economic Resiliency

Cities with a diverse set of small businesses can weather market changes more successfully and are less likely to lose their growing businesses to other cities or countries. A diverse set of artisan businesses is an important piece of this business base.

Many cities are working on "economic gardening"—the concept of growing the size and scale of existing local businesses—because these owners are most likely to stay in town and hire local residents. Cities that invest in this diversity of business and job type are likely to see less "boom and bust" since they are less reliant on one major industry. This fact is true from small town to big city. Additionally, salaries in small-scale production businesses, like artisan businesses, pay nearly double as compared to those in retail or service.[1] These businesses create jobs that fill a key gap in local economies in need of good jobs, in the process creating more equitable local communities.

Power of the Local Market

The growing movement of "Buy Local" continues to spread across the United States and provides producers with strong local markets alongside access to a global market through the Internet. More people gravitate toward unique and custom products that can be found on sites like Etsy, at pop-up events like MadeInDC, or on e-commerce platforms like Custom Made. Organizations, such as SFMade in San Francisco, strengthen the community of local producers and help them market their products locally and globally. Businesses in rural towns market beyond their immediate community to neighboring larger cities and around the world. All of these pieces can come together to add energy to a neighborhood redevelopment project.

[1]Pratt Center for Community Development, March 2015

HOW DO WE MAKE IT HAPPEN?

Community development leaders need to start thinking about artisan businesses as potential tenants during project financing and design and implement the plan all the way through marketing and long-term rollout of their project.

Although there are many details to any successful local real estate project that incorporates artisan businesses, three key areas stand out:

1. **Reach out to diverse artisan business owners to involve them from the beginning.**
   The artisan business community is the strongest asset to a neighborhood when they come from the full diversity of the community. One must work hard to engage artisans that might reflect different races and ethnicities, different tenures of business, and even different materials of production. Existing community development corporations and incoming real estate developers should invest time upfront to build partnerships in the community to help identify these businesses, and make sure to reach out to home-based businesses and immigrant populations as well from the start of the development process.

2. **Plan for artisan businesses to be a tenant from the start of the project.**
   Real estate developers who want to include artisan business tenants must underwrite their projects to include below-market production or micro-retail space from the start. The building design must consider production needs like truck loading, weight of large tools, ventilation, and safety. Micro-retail space (less than 500 square feet) for local producers can be an amazing asset but must be designed carefully.

3. **Organize programming or partner with a local entity to host regular events.**
   The neighborhood and artisan spaces will thrive when the community comes together with the artisan to market the space and the businesses to foot traffic. Building owners may need to require core business hours for micro-retail spaces to be open or select one day a week for a market or open house. Marketing and promotion both on and offline for these businesses will be key to their tenure.

The neighborhood and artisan spaces will thrive when the community comes together with the artisan to market the space and the businesses to foot traffic.

Success in equitable neighborhood redevelopment depends on a special formula of ingredients that includes residents, the city, and the private sector. Artisan businesses can be one key piece to create great places to live with wonderful places to gather and vibrant local economies.

Ilana Preuss is the founder of Recast City. She has spent nearly 20 years working with communities and businesses across the country helping them build strong places by adopting and implementing real estate and infrastructure development policies. She now focuses on connecting small-scale manufacturing and maker industries to neighborhood redevelopment and real estate opportunities.

Chapter 6

arts + community development organizations

Building through the Arts: With, for, and as Neighbors to Our Communities

BY AVIVA KAPUST

ARTS-BASED COMMUNITY DEVELOPMENT is the art of using creative collaboration to solve complex problems. Applied to issues of deep and systemic social inequality, its success relies on the willingness of the collective—artists, residents, community development groups, and members of the public-service sector—to embrace risk, to be irreverent, innovative, alternative, and challenging. When it works, arts-based community development brings out generosity and compassion in people so they can *continue* to create a better world together long after the completion of plans and the cutting of ribbons. When it works, it antiquates the unfortunate practice of conceiving, designing, and executing projects without sustained community interaction. When it works, it leaves in its wake the powerful belief that problems exist to be solved—rather than used as scapegoats for inaction or seen as impermeable barriers to upward mobility.

VILLAGE OF ARTS AND HUMANITIES—A MODEL

For more than 30 years, the Village of Arts and Humanities has been a laboratory for innovation in arts-based community development. Our legacy is steeped in the early work of founders Arthur Hall (founder of Ile Ife Black Humanitarian Center, predecessor of the Village) and Lily Yeh, who were doing creative placemaking in our community of North Central Philadelphia before "creative placemaking" was a buzz word. They believed that as artists working in the community they were as much facilitators and co-creators as they were makers and interpreters. They recognized that arts-based thinking and doing could not only influence the ongoing creation of images and environments with which we surround ourselves, but also assuage the long-term trauma in people caused by decades of oppression and disinvestment in their neighborhood.

Today's Village maintains that artists working in communities are most impactful when present over significant periods of time, much like Arthur and Lily. This approach strengthens artists' grasp on the desires and impulses of the neighborhood; positions them to effectively harness the skills and talents of individual residents; and, finally, blurs the line between artist and audience. As an arts organization that also serves as the neighborhood's de facto community development corporation (a role that includes but is not limited to spearheading efforts to revitalize the adjacent Germantown Commercial Corridor, stabilizing more than 200 vacant parcels of land for the city and providing a variety of social and technical services to the community), belief in this approach guides our practice in arts-based community development and our arts and culture work more broadly.

SPACES ARTIST-IN-RESIDENCY PROGRAM

To further our effectiveness at the intersection of arts and community development, the Village established SPACES Artist-In-Residency program, a rapid prototyping lab for arts-based projects aimed at increasing access to local information and resources, driving intentional community development outcomes, and testing positive solutions to needs and challenges unique to our neighborhood. SPACES begins with the understanding that change must be born from within the community itself, and that before change can be imagined, certainly before it can be visible in a *place*, it must first happen within *people*.

During four- to nine-month residencies, teams of visiting artists and neighborhood artists—community residents who are paid team members—engage with community and citywide stakeholders through informal and Village-facilitated dialogue, programs, or workshops in order to design and execute an original, transformative project that is rooted in art, born from the artists' relationships with the community, and realized in partnership with the community and citywide stakeholders.

When it works, it leaves in its wake the powerful belief that problems exist to be solved—rather than used as scapegoats for inaction or seen as impermeable barriers to upward mobility.

The platform serves to humanize and actualize the emotions, grievances, and fears of those who may not have another place to voice concerns. SPACES assuages the community's historic feeling of dis-belonging as residents engage in arts-driven community development projects as co-leaders, informing the projects' lasting effect by their consistent involvement in and ownership of the initiatives. The projects' stakeholders work together to creatively expose and resolve issues of social justice that tend to prevent the community envisioning its own better future. Finally, SPACES artists-in-residence live, study, and work as neighbors to their community partners, ensuring that the most vital 21st-century skill—empathy—forms the foundation of their work.

This program requires that its visiting artists must be committed to research, experimentation, and iteration; dedicated to fostering collaboration with community members; and capable of contributing extraordinary artistry and craftsmanship within their disciplines. Therefore, SPACES designed a "Call for Artists" rather than a "Call for Project Proposals." Artists from across the nation respond to one or more Community Design Principles set forth by youth/adult community residents and neighborhood stakeholders—these principles encompass the unique needs and challenges of our community.

SPACES ARTISTS RESPOND TO COMMUNITY NEED AND OPPORTUNITY

The 2014-15 inaugural cycle of SPACES welcomed three artist-in-residence cohorts, including artist/activist team Mark Strandquist and Courtney Bowles, who joined with five neighborhood artists to design and execute a project that seeks to "transform the narrative of re-entry."

In Philadelphia, one in five residents has a criminal record. In our North Central Philadelphia community, that statistic increases to two in five residents. These records create obstacles to employment, housing, education, healthcare, and social mobility, while stigmatizing and shackling people to their past. Of the 1,500 youth and families served by the Village annually, 93 percent have an incarcerated family member or neighbor. More than half of the individuals re-entering our community from prison end up back in the system within three years. People's Paper Co-op (PPC) seeks to reveal the "soul" of these statistics and to design new solutions that will create positive, lasting change. The project is exemplary of the innovative collaboration needed to remove barriers to individual and community-wide upward mobility.

PPC partners with a local, volunteer lawyer group to present free criminal record expungement clinics, where participants may clear or clean up their criminal records. Participants tear up their records, pulp them in a blender, and transform them into blank sheets of paper. On a single sheet, the participants embed their new Polaroid portraits and complete the statement, "Without my record I am..."—this becomes their "reverse mug shot." The reverse mug shots are woven into a giant paper mural comprised of pulped criminal records, human faces, and local histories.

The clinics serve as public stages upon which individuals who are disinclined to engage in civic activity join together to exercise their collective civic voice and creative power. The clinics are venues where empathy and alliances are built between strange bedfellows: lawyers, ex-offenders, politicians, artists, and law enforcement.

PPC's collaborative of ex-offenders and artists also operates a small creative business selling their handmade paper and books out of a storefront on our struggling commercial corridor, online, and at city-wide events. The proceeds are reinvested to create advocacy materials, resource guides, safe-space events, educational workshops, and to fund an internship program for women transitioning from halfway houses. Through its immediate and significant impact, PPC is now regarded as one of Philadelphia's top think tanks for local and neighborhood-based solutions that seek to mend or reinvent the broken justice system, with and for the people it is meant to serve.

RETURNING TO COMMUNITY-BASED ART, BUILDING ARTS-BASED COMMUNITY DEVELOPMENT

The work of People's Paper Co-op, the SPACES program, and the Village at-large is rooted in *intentional and meaningful interaction with the community*—the foundation of true community-based art. To achieve lasting, neighborhood-wide transformation we must also design creative collaborations between our community and outside parties who have significant existing or potential influence on the community. The success of these collaborations relies on fostering a mutual belief that communities are the most qualified experts on their challenges, needs, and wishes, and that individuals residing in our community possess abundant skill and talent that should be harnessed and amplified to make the most lasting positive change. Change must happen in people before it can happen in place—and we must not forget that our work is to move beyond only activating new thinking in the communities we serve. We must also catalyze new thinking within our respective development fields, in the practices of the people who propel these fields forward. In this way, we will build on the spark of change created by art, to a movement of change created by artists—creative thinkers—in all sectors.

Change must happen in people before it can happen in place.

Aviva Kapust is the executive director of the Village of Arts and Humanities. She is also a graphic designer, youth educator, and advocate for equitable revitalization in underserved urban communities. Before working at the Village, Kapust worked as a designer and creative director at advertising agencies in New York and San Francisco, and as an adjunct professor at Temple University.

How Can a CDC (or the City) Effectively Work with Artists to Drive Revitalization?

BY KIRA STRONG

OVERVIEW

We at People's Emergency Center Community Development Corporation in West Philadelphia, like any entity working to revitalize its neighborhood, are fortunate to have many local inherent assets and homegrown partners. Our work had traditionally focused on affordable housing, but as we have expanded our programming over the past ten years to include broader neighborhood revitalization strategies, we have recognized the number, value, and needs of the many artists who live in our neighborhood. Some of these artists were born here while others were drawn by inexpensive housing, proximity to local universities, and great transit. By engaging with this diverse artist population at local meetings and public forums, we opened a dialogue with them, which led us to pursue a study to pinpoint their most pressing needs.

These findings uncovered a common fear of being pushed out of the area due to rising prices caused by local development, and the desire to have greater connectedness among artists and arts and culture groups. They also led us to create affordable live-work housing for artists and to think in broader terms about how to best serve this population.

NEIGHBORHOOD TIME EXCHANGE: A UNIQUE ARTIST RESIDENCY
In response, we recently collaborated with the City of Philadelphia's Mural Arts Program, the City of Philadelphia's Office of Arts Culture and Creative Economy, and Broken City Lab, from Vancouver, Canada, to create the Neighborhood Time Exchange (NTE). This project focused on the concept of having resident artists trade paid studio time in exchange for answering "service requests" submitted by local community members. It was installed in

a vacant storefront on our local commercial corridor, at the convergence of four different neighborhoods.

We solicited the help of local artists and arts organizations to form an advisory committee to provide feedback on the call for artists and select the artists who would participate in the residency. We determined that it was critical for the residency not only to include non-Philadelphia artists who would bring a different perspective to local issues and challenges, but also to have a specific focus on local Philadelphia artists. Applications came in from as far away as Egypt and Ireland. Artists diverse in age, gender, race, and geography who work in a range of media were selected by the advisory committee.

The artist residencies were structured to have four artists on-site at a time for three months each. Each grouping included an artist from West Philadelphia, a Philadelphia artist from anywhere in the city, and two artists from other parts of the state, country, or world.

The Respect Your Block artwork was created in Philadelphia, Pennsylvania, for the community association Women of Belmont as part of the Neighborhood Time Exchange project.
PHOTO BY ALBERT YEE

LESSONS LEARNED

We quickly learned that **three months is not long enough.** Many artists felt that by the time they established relationships within the community it was time to leave, and the number of service requests the community submitted far outweighed the artists' ability to answer them. When we launched this, much was unknown about how this would all transpire. We had no idea if anyone would walk into the studio space, or request anything at all; if the service requests would call upon skill sets not available, cause controversy, or stir interest in art more specifically; or if the project would even resonate in any way.

It was a **challenge for artists to balance personal studio time with community service hours.** Each artist's workload was determined by how many requests were made and what level of commitment he or she made to each. Our first group of artists felt enormous pressure to complete every service request, leaving them little time to focus on their own personal studio work. We addressed this by encouraging artists to give their personal work the attention it deserved, and to feel comfortable saying "no" as requests came in.

The **delineation between public and private** can blur not only in time but in physical space as well. While the storefront, 4017 Lancaster Avenue, served as a hub for community members to present project ideas, the demarcation of a public storefront space was quickly viewed as a necessity to ensure that personal studio areas were not trampled through. We installed a curtain system to allow for more privacy in studio spaces, and worked diligently to enforce our scheduled open hours.

We benefited from having **strong project management** across the organizations leading the initiative; **input from our local arts community** throughout the process, especially at the front end; and **orientation weekends** to introduce visiting artists to the community. Having ample open storefront hours and events and answering community residents' questions in an effort to communicate the Neighborhood Time Exchange presence were also key components to success.

> By welcoming visitors into the neighborhood, we have opened a dialogue that has allowed us to share the beauty and challenges of our specific part of West Philadelphia.

CONCLUSION

With the project now complete (with anticipation of a re-start in spring 2016), we could not be more thrilled with all that it has enabled. The majority of the projects requested had some form of civic engagement or education component. We had an artist help create a quilted photo curtain for a local church commemorating their 100th year, and a set of artists in different cohorts piggyback on each other in responding to a group of local women who requested help in communicating local pride and beautifying a long-time eyesore of a vacant lot. Another artist responded to a service request from a local school that had no way to record their students' performances, which turned into a project teaching students media skills with donated recording equipment, which enables the students to continue long after the artist has left.

In addition to the success of the concept of trading personal art-making time for community revitalization and engagement projects, the attention it has drawn to what a creative approach can bring to a challenge is crucial. By welcoming visitors into the neighborhood, we have opened a dialogue that has allowed us to share the beauty and challenges of our specific part of West Philadelphia with those previously unfamiliar with it. We are now busy strategizing how Neighborhood Time Exchange can live on for a second year. One local school has already requested an on-site NTE artist for the coming school year. Most importantly, however, we have benefited from the creativity and engagement of our community members and our local and visiting artists.

Kira Strong is the vice president of community and economic development at People's Emergency Center in Philadelphia, Pennsylvania. She has overseen community development activities for five target neighborhoods in West Philadelphia, including $43 million in real estate and economic developments.

Embracing Arts as a Key Community Development Strategy

OPA-LOCKA, FL

FOUNDED IN THE 1920S BY AVIATION PIONEER Glenn Curtiss, the city of Opa-locka, Florida, got its start in a time of prosperity and possibility. Over the years, though, the city has faced a series of challenges, sluggish economy, and soaring crime rates. Of the 15,500 residents in Opa-locka today, 31 percent now live below the Federal Poverty Level, and the median family income is $19,000. The Opa-locka Community Development Corporation (OLCDC) was founded in 1980 to address the distressed unemployment conditions in North Miami-Dade County and help with overall revitalization initiatives for the city of Opa-locka.

The Magnolia North neighborhood has long been isolated from the surrounding city by a set of imposing barriers put in place in the 1980s, originally designed to stem the flow of drugs that scourged the area during that time. Though citywide demographics are about 65 percent African-American and 35 percent Latino residents, the Magnolia North neighborhood consists mainly of African-American families who have lived there since before the barricades were put in place or are struggling households in need of temporary and low-cost housing. Thankfully the drug scourge of the 1980s and '90s is under control, but the metal barricades have stayed long after their aims were accomplished, leaving the area disjointed from the surrounding area. In order for the city to move forward, the OLCDC needed to create strategic plans that could address both the existing barriers and the overall larger physical fabric of the neighborhood.

The city and the OLCDC set about to invest in a comprehensive strategy of housing creation, public space development, and public art. In place of the barricades, OLCDC imagined public spaces that would offer a different message. "You have to dispel this perception of a tough area," said Opa-locka Vice Mayor Joseph Kelley. To do this, OLCDC hired four artist teams: Roberto Behar and Rosario Marquardt designed an open-air community room as a terminus to the future Duval Market Street; Gale Fulton Ross conceived a steel sculpture to be assembled by community members; architects Jennifer Bonner, Christian Stayner, and Germane Barnes related designs to convert foreclosed houses into sites for community spaces ("public houses") and microenterprises; and landscape architect Walter Hood designed public spaces that connect the urban landscape, take into account the natural environment, and integrate recycled automobile parts. Collectively, these projects fell under the umbrella project called Community Gateways. Within these efforts, the OLCDC recognized that art had to be used strategically as part of their larger community development goals and not as a stand-alone effort.

Ali Baba Community Paint Day, in which community members revitalize a barren stretch of Ali Baba Avenue in Opa-locka, Florida, with a fresh coat of paint.
PHOTO COURTESY OF OPA-LOCKA COMMUNITY DEVELOPMENT CORPORATION

As with any successful urban initiative, Community Gateways was the result of a coalition of public and private partner organizations. The City of Opa-locka was integral, creating and amending zoning policies to support the role of public art in urban development. The project also benefited from an advisory panel comprised of Perez Art Museum Miami Associate Curator Rene Morales and members from the Art in Public Places program at the Miami-Dade County Department of Cultural Affairs. As a way to encourage community involvement, the OLCDC worked closely with the county art liaison and the city's planning department to review public input into the project.

Managing the project was an intricate and sometimes daunting task, particularly for an organization unfamiliar with arts management. Central to their strategy was bringing on the right people to serve as advisors to the process. Allowing the artists to focus on their work, OLCDC worked to secure the funding and administration, including zoning work required for open space development, and pushed for an overlay amendment that would allow for live/work residential spaces. A 2011 Choice Neighborhoods Initiative Planning Grant from HUD and 2012 HUD Sustainable Communities Challenge grant allowed for a sustainability planning effort that allowed the city the chance to continue refining the project.

The project has had important tangible effects on the neighborhood and city and provided community members with a vision for the future. The four proposed artworks are in different stages of funding and implementation, though OLCDC is committed to seeing all move forward. These artworks were strategically chosen to attract further support for future parts of the plan. While OLCDC has identified a goal of tripling the population of the Magnolia North neighborhood, it understands it will need to consider a long-term time horizon for the art to have that measurable effect.

One of the most difficult issues of the project was getting residents to overcome their sense of apathy during the various planning processes. Having been subject to years of planning with little to show for it, many residents did not see the current planning efforts as much different. With the commitment of individual artists who repeatedly sought community input, residents became increasingly involved in the different projects. One project artist, architect Germane Barnes, moved to the area to help see his project come to fruition. Using art and design to help convert buildings into sites where small micro-enterprises could happen—such as cutting hair or baking—Barnes worked through a series of community activities, including building a new park, to help renovate public spaces and buildings.

Developing Communities through Creative Placemaking

BY ERIK TAKESHITA

OVER THE LAST DECADE, MAYORS, DEVELOPERS, and other community leaders have increasingly recognized the power of arts and culture to transform the physical landscape of neighborhoods and generate economic gains. Many of them were inspired by Richard Florida's seminal work, *The Rise of the Creative Class*[1] or Ann Markusen and Anne Gadwa's white paper for the National Endowment for the Arts (NEA), *Creative Placemaking*.[2] In haste to generate these benefits, what can be overlooked is how creative placemaking transforms—for better or worse—the social fabric of a community.

I have spent most of my career supporting community development. This work might be a group of neighbors or businesses coming together to improve their neighborhood; a religious institution working to improve its surrounding community; or a community development corporation focused on building housing, helping with job training, or supporting small business development. Regardless of if it is volunteer-driven or professional, religious-based or secular, community developers share a common goal of improving the lives of existing residents and businesses. In short, they want to help *people and places prosper*.[3]

[1] Florida, R. *The Rise of the Creative Class: And How It's Transforming Work, Leisure, Community, and Everyday Life*. Perseus Book Group. 2002.

[2] Markusen, A. and A. Gadwa. *Creative Placemaking*. National Endowment for the Arts. 2010.

[3] See http://www.tclisc.org/

Group engaged in Feast of the Street activities in Phoenix, Arizona.
PHOTO BY ANDREW PIELAGE PHOTOGRAPHY

Community developers want physical and economic development, but they are sensitive to the danger of involuntary displacement of existing residents and businesses, a process sometimes known as "gentrification." They understand displacement can be either financial—current residents and businesses can no longer afford to live or do business in the neighborhood or town—or psychological, where people no longer recognize the community as "their own."

Community developers realize creative placemaking can be a powerful tool for physical improvement and economic transformation of communities, but also know for it to be truly community development, their efforts must support and reflect a community's cultural development while also mitigating the potential unintended consequences of the very physical change and economic growth they seek to advance.

FINANCIAL DISPLACEMENT

Community developers want to improve the physical landscape and increase economic activity in their communities. They also, however, recognize that while increasing property values and attracting new investment are good things, they can also "price out" incumbent residents and businesses, resulting in unintended financial displacement. Community developers recognize and appreciate this tension of wanting development without displacement.

Authentic community cultural development must be community-driven.

To help mitigate the risk of unintended financial displacement, creative placemaking efforts can be coupled with other more traditional housing and business development strategies. For example, efforts can be taken to help artists, residents, and businesses acquire their homes or the properties where they do business to help insulate them from potential rent increases, while also helping them build wealth as property values rise. Efforts can also be made to help artists and other non-arts-related businesses take steps to capitalize on new traffic to the neighborhood by becoming more "visitor-ready" through things such as new signage, improved customer service or merchandising, looking at supply chain and inventory issues, and adjusting pricing to maximize profits.

PSYCHOLOGICAL/SPIRITUAL DISPLACEMENT

While having the financial means to stay if one wants is critical, it is equally important to community developers that artists, residents, and businesses are able to continue to recognize a neighborhood or town as "their own." Fortunately, for community developers, the very mechanism that can incentivize physical transformation and economic gains for communities—creative placemaking—can also be used for community cultural development that can help communities maintain an authentic sense of identity.

Authentic community cultural development must be community-driven. Creative placemaking is not value-neutral. Through creative placemaking, individuals endow a space with certain values—theirs. If the people driving the creative placemaking efforts are from the community, it will necessarily reflect their hopes, dreams, and desires; their values. If, however, creative placemaking efforts are driven by people from outside the community, these efforts will, again necessarily, reflect values coming from outside the existing community. Because creative placemaking inherently reflects the worldview and values of those initiating and leading it, community developers know that it is critical that the people who live in a town or neighborhood are the ones driving the changes in their community.

CONCLUSION

It is clear that creative placemaking can lead to physical and economic development in neighborhoods and towns of all shapes and sizes. However, for this work to be considered community development, it must be community-driven and authentically reflect the unique culture of incumbent residents and businesses. Creative placemaking focused on community development must support community-driven cultural development to ensure residents and businesses recognize the neighborhood or town "as their own"—a place that reflects their values and makes them feel welcome. These community-driven creative placemaking efforts need to also be linked to more traditional community development endeavors such as long-term affordability and building income and assets to ensure existing residents and businesses that want to stay can afford to do so.

Erik Takeshita is the community creativity portfolio director for the Bush Foundation. He has more than 20 years of experience working at the intersection of community development and the arts, and is nationally recognized for managing high-impact initiatives that express a community's unique culture through the arts.

Reimagining Vacant Spaces through Temporary Art Projects

PHOENIX, AZ

THE CAPITAL OF ARIZONA, PHOENIX is a city of nearly 1.5 million people, with 4.5 million in its metropolitan region. Its downtown area is a mix of buildings and programs—a central business district combined with single-family detached homes, museums, and government buildings. The city's 2004 strategic plan, Downtown Phoenix: A Strategic Vision and Blueprint for the Future, called for more retail space, new jobs, and a focus on the arts. In 2008, when the light rail system was completed to connect the downtown to the entire metropolitan region, the area's emerging identity as a new cultural spine, linking new cultural organizations and sites with established ones like the Phoenix Art Museum, Heard Museum, and Burton Barr Central Library, was bolstered. Also the light rail corridor connected to Roosevelt Row, the city's downtown creative district.

The 2008 mortgage crisis brought a rising tide of foreclosures and empty storefronts to the state, including on Roosevelt Row. In an attempt to combat these issues, the city developed a number of programs and activities to occupy these vacant spaces and help the downtown area to continue to grow. As part of this effort, the Phoenix Office of Arts and Culture (POAC) created a two-year arts initiative titled Cultural Connections. Based on a previous successful Roosevelt Row program A.R.T.S. (Adaptive Re-Use of Temporary Space) and Mayor Greg Stanton's Phoenix ReNew's Program, Cultural Connections provided free public art events and temporary public art installations to animate vacant spaces on the Row, bolster the developing cultural district, and enhance the broader public experience of the downtown area.

Cultural Connection project partners included the Phoenix Arts and Culture Commission, a group of citizen volunteers appointed by the mayor that work to advise and approve the city's public art

**Community members
working on the public
art project Ground
Cover in Phoenix,
Arizona.**
PHOTO COURTESY OF
THE ARTIST,
ANN MORTON

programs; Roosevelt Row Community Development Corporation
(CDC); and the Arizona State University Art Museum. Roosevelt
Row CDC helped to ensure the project was tightly connected with
the neighborhood while Arizona State University Art Museum
assisted with artist recruitment and planning workshops. ASU Art
Museum's commitment to the neighborhood and its organizational
capacity were a boon.

One of the artists selected through a 2012 Call for Ideas was artist
Ann Morton. Her temporary project, Ground Cover, employed
nearly 600 volunteers to make 300 knitted, crocheted, woven, or
quilted blankets that when put together created a 117 ft. X 50 ft.
"ground cover." When viewed from above, the blankets combined
to create a colossal image of lush desert blooms, each blanket
square a "pixel" in the overall image. After installation, the blankets
were given to a variety of agencies serving the homeless, who in
turn gave them to individuals in need of cover.

Overall, Cultural Connections in tandem with Phoenix's other public art programs has decreased area blight, improved pedestrian traffic in the downtown area, and increased the number of Phoenix artists with commissions. It has brokered new community partnerships and instigated conversations about art and public space in the local media. Additionally, many of the projects, including Ground Cover, have served as platforms for conversations about local needs and other local socioeconomic challenges. Finally, Cultural Connections has led to further creative placemaking efforts in the area; in 2014, Roosevelt Row began construction on a new streetscape to further improve the neighborhood's design and landscape.

Moving from Theory to Practice: Exploring the Uptake of the Arts by Community Development Practitioners

BY LYZ CRANE

MANY YEARS AGO, MY FIRST INTERNSHIP in the field of community development was working at Partners for Livable Communities updating a database of more than 700 best practices in livability. I was blown away by how many of the examples leveraged the creative assets of artists and arts organizations to help communities drive comprehensive strategies to create places where people could thrive.

The idea that the arts have a role to play in community development is not new, and the base of connected practitioners pushing the boundaries of arts-based community development strategies continues to grow. Moreover, across the country the community development sector is moving toward comprehensive strategies that leverage the combined strength of housing, health, economic development, transportation, and other sectors to take a systems-based approach to building healthy communities that are filled with opportunity for their residents.

Because of the move toward working in a more comprehensive way, many community development organizations are beginning to ask questions not just about how to deliver services and develop buildings, but about how to build community in a broad sense. The arts can be an effective catalyst to asking questions and developing strategies around how people feel, gather, vision, process change, and experience their communities.

Zuni Youth Enrichment Project asks the Zuni community about potential uses for a new public space.
PHOTO COURTESY OF ARTPLACE AMERICA

Yet, the arts sector is still often left out of these comprehensive conversations. Many community planning and development organizations still struggle with taking those first few steps to reach out to the arts sector. During a recent grant application process, we asked those organizations why they had not formed collaborations with the arts in the past. Some of the most commonly cited reasons beyond time, staff capacity, and financial resources included:

• the focus on specific metrics such as housing units built, jobs created, or services provided that did not allow for what folks thought might be more "fuzzy" or "in-between" outcomes;
• limited experience and knowledge of the local arts sector or limited understanding of artistic practice; and
• lack of knowledge of viable models that may be applicable for their community or organization's way of working.

WHAT DO COMMUNITY PLANNING AND DEVELOPMENT ORGANIZATIONS NEED TO KNOW?

ArtPlace America is a ten-year collaboration among a number of foundations, federal agencies, and financial institutions that works to position arts and culture as a core sector of comprehensive community planning and development. ArtPlace focuses its work on creative placemaking, which describes projects in which art plays an intentional and integrated role in place-based community planning and development.

To address this question of just what community planning and development organizations need to know, ArtPlace America created the Community Development Investments (CDI) program. CDI recognizes that many organizations could benefit from some guided thinking in getting started, so it provides three million dollars of flexible funding along with technical assistance to participating community planning and development organizations. Those organizations are then able to consider how the arts can add value through both creative processes and arts-based projects. This journey of organizational change and new project development is being documented to help other similar organizations learn step-by-step how to approach relationship-building around common goals with the arts sector and demystify common challenges that arise in the process.

In launching this process, the organizations have been asking three driving questions:

- What are the big questions in our community that reach across many needs and lines of work?
- What is it that artists and the arts sector can do?
- How can they do it and add value within the context of community development?

WHAT ARE THE BIG QUESTIONS IN OUR COMMUNITIES?

The CDI participants range from community development corporations to a housing authority to a parks conservancy to a medical facility to a tribal youth development organization, and are all over the country in communities of all sizes—from Anchorage, Alaska, to Jackson, Mississippi, to rural Minnesota. They are each a core part of their community's planning and development infrastructure, having to respond to the macro- and micro-economic, social, and political forces at work in their communities, develop lines of work and projects that address some of the most pressing needs and challenges their communities face, and advance a vision for the future. Some of the specific questions these organizations have decided to tackle as critical to their communities' futures include how the arts can help them to:

- Better reflect the values, cultures, and identities of increasingly diverse populations in new housing and commercial development;
- Be more inclusive of many identities and voices in community planning and visioning processes;
- Build community strength and power to exert community control over a rapidly changing neighborhood;
- Better welcome, serve, and integrate new immigrant populations;
- Improve health outcomes through active lifestyles and the active use of public space; and
- Create public spaces that serve to enhance social cohesion and economic development.

These questions are not unique to these organizations or these communities, but they are each opportunities for the arts to knit together social, economic, and physical investments that can drive a positive vision for a community.

There is also a growing field of social and civic practice artists who focus on producing work in collaboration with communities and other individuals.

WHAT IS IT THAT THE ARTS CAN DO?

An oft-repeated statement by ArtPlace America is to remind practitioners that every community has artists, culture bearers, and creative people who have something to contribute. Much of the initial learning each participating organization is doing is around understanding the infrastructure of the arts sector (everything from local arts councils to anchor arts institutions to college art departments), how to find artists (both by networking through local organizations and using census and other datasets), and how to understand various kinds of artistic practice.

For those outside of the arts sector, this latter topic can be eye-opening. Often they know about the familiar idea of an artist working in a studio, producing art products that may be shared or sold or even presented in public spaces and places. However, there is also a growing field of social and civic practice artists who focus on producing work in collaboration with communities and other individuals, so that their artistic process is informed by and informs planning, people, and public spaces in a broader sense. These collaborative artists can be particularly valuable partners for community development projects and processes. Local arts organizations, arts councils, and cultural departments can be effective partners in helping to identify artists who may be interested in collaborating on a community vision.

HOW CAN ARTISTS AND THE ARTS SECTOR ADD VALUE INTO COMMUNITY DEVELOPMENT PROCESSES?

There is a long history of studying the ways in which art manifests visibly in communities through either temporary or permanent public art, events/festivals, branding, and art spaces or institutions and how this can positively contribute to the experience of a place.

However the arts can also do so much more. Community planning and development happens in a constant feedback loop of engagement, prioritization, execution, and reflection. Just as every community has creative individuals, every phase of community planning and development processes can benefit from deploying arts-based strategies and projects.

For example, the arts sector can help:

- Understand and access community members who are not traditionally included in community development projects;
- Better and more creatively engage and empower community members in identifying community challenges and opportunities;
- Contribute to design, planning, and implementation of projects; and
- Better evaluate and communicate what's working or changing in communities.

In looking at not just *what* they are trying to accomplish, but *how* they are doing their work, the CDI participants are rapidly discovering that the arts sector can be a uniquely valuable ally in improving outcomes across the board.

Examples of how to involve the arts in various community development phases:

- **Understand and access a community:** Map the cultural lives of community members to identify nodes of civic activity. For example, Project Willowbrook in Los Angeles: http://lacountyarts.org/willowbrook/
- **Engage and empower community members to articulate needs:** Deploy creative strategies to uncover interests, needs, and values. For example, Pop Up Meeting in St. Paul: http://publicartstpaul.org/project/popup
- **Design, planning, and implementation:** Involve artists in reimagining how public space looks, feels, and functions. For example, Santo Domingo Heritage Trail Arts Project: http://greenfiretimes.com/2015/07/update-the-santo-domingo-heritage-trail-arts-project/
- **Evaluate and communicate:** Engage artists to creatively tell the stories of how communities are evolving and changing. For example, Imagine Fergus Falls: http://imaginefergusfalls.tumblr.com/about

MOVING FORWARD: EXPANDING AND DEEPENING IMPACT

As the community development field evolves, it is becoming clearer that projects that do not at least try to address the "stuff in the middle" of housing, health, economy, and services are not sufficient. By their very nature, the arts can offer context-dependent, innovative, culturally relevant, and meaningful solutions to creating connected, healthy, and opportunity-filled communities. In being open to asking new questions, building new relationships, and trying new ways of working, the community development field has the opportunity to both expand and deepen the potential impact organizations can have in a place.

Lyz Crane is deputy director at ArtPlace America. She has previously worked with ArtHome, which helps artists to build assets and equity through financial literacy, and Partners for Livable Communities, which supports the livability of communities by promoting strategies around quality of life, economic development, and social equity.

Creative Placemaking: Toward a Sustainable Practice

BY MARIA ROSARIO JACKSON

FOR MORE THAN 20 YEARS AND FROM various vantage points I have been involved in documenting, examining, assessing, and facilitating the integration of arts and culture into (1) conceptions of communities where all people, and especially historically marginalized populations, can thrive, and (2) strategies for comprehensive community revitalization. For the past few years, there has been a revival of interest in the interconnected nature of urban conditions and the importance of place in determining life outcomes. That is, there is increasing recognition that the characteristics of the places where people live have implications for long-term conditions related to health, education, economic attainment, and other considerations. Moreover, there is recognition that simple siloed approaches to the interrelated challenges of many communities are inadequate. One can't address health challenges without addressing housing and environmental issues. One can't address housing without addressing employment. One can't address employment without addressing education, and so on. So what is the role of arts and culture in this context? In 2010, the National Endowment for the Arts, together with philanthropic leadership, asserted interest in creative placemaking—originally discussed as activity in which "partners from public, private, nonprofit, and community sectors strategically shape the physical and social character of a neighborhood, town, city, or region around arts and cultural activities."[1] As creative placemaking has gained more traction, variations of the original and other definitions of the term have emerged.

---

[1] Markusen, A. and A. Gadwa. *Creative Placemaking*. National Endowment for the Arts. 2010.

SO WHAT IS CREATIVE PLACEMAKING?

Evident from some of the examples presented in this compilation of writings, creative placemaking can have many different manifestations in challenged communities, including artists involved in community planning—helping to frame issues and devise solutions as well as helping to bring forward community perspectives and voice; residents lending their creativity and imagination in community-engaged design processes; collective art-making activity that leads to stronger social cohesion; economic development strategies focused on creative enterprises and capitalizing on residents' creativity and cultural assets; artful improvements in the built environment, including transformation of blight, new buildings and spaces that reflect the cultural sensibilities of a community, and activity explicitly intended to create a different or alternative narrative of place through all manner of expression—writing, visual art, design, music, theater, foodways, community ritual, and entrepreneurship.

Creative placemaking, in my opinion, is another manifestation of civic engagement and democracy—people exercising their right and obligation to be present, step up, and shape the communities in which they live. At its best, I think, creative placemaking is based on the following premises:

- The creativity of community residents and the unique features of a place (e.g., physical characteristics, history, cultural traditions, etc.) are community assets from which to build.
- Artists, designers, tradition bearers have key roles to play throughout and at critical junctures in change processes—helping to frame community issues and devise solutions.
- Arts and cultural activity can have intrinsic value as well as instrumental value concurrently (it does not have to be either/or).
- Preservation and innovation are both important, can co-exist, and even be synergistic.
- Creative process is as important as creative product and must be valued.
- An arts intervention is not a silver bullet; it is an important element of a necessarily multipronged approach to complex situations.
- Care is taken to ensure that existing residents of low-income communities benefit equitably from community change.

Is creative placemaking activity new? No. Not always. While certainly not common enough in conventional urban planning and community development practices, there are important examples of artists, designers, and tradition bearers that have been major contributors to community improvement initiatives long before anyone was using the term creative placemaking. Longstanding work at AS220 in Providence, Rhode Island; Project Row Houses in Houston, Texas; City of Philadelphia Mural Arts Program; East Los Angeles Community Corporation; Chinatown Community Development Center in San Francisco; Ashe Cultural Arts Center in New Orleans; Appalshop in Whitesburg, Kentucky; the Wing Luke Museum in Seattle; and several others are such examples. Practitioners in all of these examples have had to step out of their comfort zone and pave the path for new ways of collaborating across professional areas of expertise. They have had to learn new terminology, juggle and negotiate sometimes competing standards of success, and they have struggled to describe their work in its fullness—how it is relevant to multiple interests and how it often does not fit neatly into pre-existing categories and paradigms. None of that is altogether new.

A significant part of the work ahead has to do with reimagining long-standing structures and ways of working.

HEADING TOWARD A SUSTAINABLE PRACTICE OF CREATIVE PLACEMAKING

What is new, and tremendously important, is (1) the growing intentional focus on arts, culture, and design as critical to good planning and community development and also increasing interest in what art, culture, and design have to offer from other policy areas such as health, transportation, and public safety, among others; (2) an increasing demand for understanding what practices are most effective for improving communities and achieving more equitable outcomes; and (3) concern for pipeline and the next generation of artists, designers, tradition bearers, community developers, urban planners, and others concerned with neighborhoods and vulnerable populations—those who will integrate arts, culture, and design in community revitalization initiatives as a matter of course.

As someone who has been long concerned with the themes now getting attention through this focus on creative placemaking, I am encouraged. But I am also mindful that for this integration of art, culture, and design into concepts of equitable, good places to live and sound strategies of community revitalization, other significant changes must be afoot. Methods and metrics for assessing quality of life have to be inclusive of broad interpretations of arts, culture, and design. Progress in community revitalization cannot only be assessed in terms of economic development when we know that other qualities of communities also matter. For policy siloes, including arts and culture, to become more connected and capable of making positive impacts on complex situations in communities, we have to acknowledge that a significant part of the work ahead has to do with reimagining long-standing structures and ways of working—leaving familiar environments and patterns of behavior and developing the validation systems that reward innovation, risk taking, and what sometimes by necessity is slow, iterative, and even tedious work as entities that have not collaborated before find their way. Last, we must address with urgency the conditions of vulnerable populations facing persistent adversity, while at the same time, exercising the patience that is required when a fundamental and enduring paradigm shift is necessary.

Resources:

http://as220.org
http://projectrowhouses.org
http://www.muralarts.org
http://www.elacc.org
http://www.chinatowncdc.org
http://www.ashecac.org/main/
https://www.appalshop.org
http://www.wingluke.org
http://kresge.org/programs/arts-culture
http://www.artplaceamerica.org

Jackson, M.R. "What are the Makings of a Healthy Community?" *The Role of Artists and the Arts in Creative Placemaking*. Goethe Institut. 2014.

Jackson, M.R. *Building Community: Making Space for Art*. Leveraging Investments in Creativity (LINC) and the Urban Institute. 2011.

Jackson, M.R. "Artist's Hybrid Work Challenges Old Ways of Evaluating Quality and Impact." *Metro Trends Blog*. The Urban Institute. 2011.

Maria Rosario Jackson, PhD, is senior advisor to the arts and culture program at the Kresge Foundation and a member of the NEA's National Council on the Arts. She is a leading expert in the fields of urban planning, comprehensive community revitalization, and arts and culture.

Credits

November 2016

National Endowment for the Arts
400 7th Street, SW
Washington, DC 20506
202-682-5400
arts.gov

Published by the NEA Office of Public Affairs

Editors: Jason Schupbach and Don Ball
Co-editors: Katryna Carter, Jenna Moran, and Bryan McEntire

Design by Fuszion

ISBN 978-0-692-78289-7

Library of Congress Cataloging-in-Publication Data

Names: Schupbach, Jason, 1975- editor. | Ball, Don, 1964- editor. | National
    Endowment for the Arts. Office of Public Affairs, publisher.
Title: How to do creative placemaking : an action-oriented guide to arts in
    community development.
Other titles: Action-oriented guide to arts in community development
Description: Washington, DC : NEA Office of Public Affairs, 2016. | Includes
    bibliographical references.
Identifiers: LCCN 2016043772 | ISBN 9780692782897
Subjects: LCSH: Arts and society—United States. | Community
    development—United States. | Public spaces—United
    States—Planning—Citizen participation. | Community arts projects—United
    States.
Classification: LCC NX180.S6 H69 2016 | DDC 701/.03—dc23 | SUDOC NF 2.2:P
    69/3
LC record available at https://lccn.loc.gov/2016043772

202-682-5496 Voice/TTY (a device for individuals who are deaf or hearing-impaired)

 Individuals who do not use conventional print materials may contact the Arts Endowment's Accessibility Office at 202-682-5532 to obtain this publication in an alternate format.

This publication is available free of charge in print or PDF format at arts.gov, the website of the National Endowment for the Arts.

Cover: In July 2015, Lakota teenager Elizabeth Eagle demonstrated fancy shawl dancing during the Cheyenne River Youth Project's inaugural RedCan graffiti jam at the innovative Waniyetu Wowapi (Winter Count) Art Park on South Dakota's Cheyenne River Sioux Reservation.
PHOTO BY RICHARD STEINBERGER COURTESY OF THE CHEYENNE RIVER YOUTH PROJECT

About the NEA

THE NATIONAL ENDOWMENT FOR THE ARTS was established by Congress in 1965 as an independent federal agency whose funding and support gives Americans the opportunity to participate in the arts, exercise their imaginations, and develop their creative capacities. Through partnerships with state arts agencies, local leaders, other federal agencies, and the philanthropic sector, the NEA supports arts learning, affirms and celebrates America's rich and diverse cultural heritage, and extends its work to promote equal access to the arts inevery community across America.

Case studies come from the Exploring Our Town microsite on the National Endowment for the Arts website: **arts.gov/exploring-our-town**